Christmas
CRAFTING *In No Time*

Christmas
CRAFTING In No Time

50 step-by-step projects and inspirational ideas

CLARE YOUNGS

CICO BOOKS

LONDON NEW YORK

Published in 2011 by CICO Books
An imprint of Ryland Peters & Small Ltd
20–21 Jockey's Fields   519 Broadway, 5th Floor
London WC1R 4BW   New York, NY 10012

www.cicobooks.com

10 9 8 7 6 5 4 3 2 1

Text © Clare Youngs 2011
Design and photography © CICO Books 2011

A CIP catalog record for this book is available from the Library
of Congress and the British Library.

ISBN 978 1 907563 78 2

Printed in China

Copy editor: Katie Hardwicke
Designer: Christine Wood
Photographers: Claire Richardson, James Gardiner, and Kate Davis
Stylists: Clare Youngs and Sophie Martell
Illustrator: Michael Hill

Contents

Introduction

There is no better time to get creative than at Christmas. Trimming the tree, decking the hall, setting the Christmas dinner table—all present wonderful opportunities to get crafty and create a sparkling, warm, and welcoming festive home.

There is something magical about the festive season. Unpacking the decorations evokes memories of Christmases past and stirs all the feelings of wonder and excitement that we felt as children. It is a time to take a break from our hectic lifestyles and enjoy the simpler things in life, like spending time with our friends and family.

Making decorations together is all part of that special time. One of my family's prettiest trees was created in a Christmas away from home, with a tree made from twigs and leaves dragged from the woods and festooned with homemade decorations created from paper, twigs, and ribbons. Children love to be involved with the preparations, whether transforming

the home into a winter wonderland or helping out in the kitchen in the days leading up to Christmas. You'll find several projects in the following pages that you can sit and make together, and many that will be loved and treasured as gifts for them to discover under the tree or spilling from hand-stitched stockings.

It is thoroughly enjoyable spending time making gorgeous gifts for loved ones. Gift wrap, greetings cards, sumptuous and stylish table settings with individual place names and handmade crackers, are all personal touches that your friends and family will really appreciate, too, and you will have the immense satisfaction of having created something stunningly beautiful with your own hands.

So get the children involved, put on some Christmas music, get stuck in, and create a truly individual and totally gorgeous homemade Christmas!

CHAPTER ONE

Decorations

Silver flower wreath

This stunning mirrored card wreath makes a stylish alternative to more traditional Christmas decorations and would make a striking focal point in a contemporary setting. Make some extra flowers and scatter them along the center of the dining table—set among glowing candles, they will reflect and shimmer in the changing light.

materials

Tracing paper and card

Pencil

Scissors

4 sheets of mirrored silver card

Craft knife

Cutting mat

Blunt knife

Piece of foam board

Glue

1 Copy the petal and flower center templates on page 165 onto tracing paper and transfer the shapes onto a piece of card (see page 146). Cut the shapes out to use as templates.

2 Place the petal template on the back of the mirrored card and draw around it to make rows of petals. You need 60 in total and you should be able to get approx. 17 on a standard-sized sheet. Cut out the petals. Draw ten flower center pieces and cut them out.

3 Lay out six petals in a flower shape, so that the petals are equally spaced and the ends completely overlap each other. Make a small slit in the top petal with a craft knife, using the template as a guide.

4 Remove the top petal and put it to one side. On the petal beneath, you will see an impression of the slit you made from the first petal. Use this as a guide to cut a slit in the second petal. Continue, making a small slit in each petal. The position of the slit will move diagonally as you go through the petals. When laying them to one side, keep the petals in the correct order, to help when you slot them together in step 6.

5 Go over each slit with the craft knife to enlarge the slit to approx. ⅟₁₆in. (1mm) wide. Score a line above each slit with a blunt knife, across the width of the petal, and bend the petal upward.

6 Take a center piece and slot the petals on one by one in reverse order, to make a flower. Repeat steps 3—6 to make ten flowers in total.

7 Draw a circle with a diameter of approx. 13½in. (34cm) on the foam board—find a bowl or large plate to draw around. Then draw a circle within that approx. 10½in. (27cm) in diameter. Using the craft knife, carefully cut out the inner circle, then cut out the outer circle to make a ring. Position the flowers all around the ring and stick them down with strong, quick-drying glue. You can hang your wreath using tack or thread a loop of silver cord around the ring to make a hanging loop.

Silk and sequinned fish

I am always on the lookout for unusual Christmas decorations and like to add one or two to my collection every year. I have a few beautiful Indian decorations, embroidered with silver and gold, which have inspired me to create these gorgeous silk fish. Use the brightest colors you can find, and embellish the fish with sequins, beads, and glittery tassels, which will catch the light as they sway and turn.

materials

Tracing paper

Pencil

Scissors

Silk fabric in various colors

Selection of sequins, ribbons, and glittery embellishments

Sewing needle and matching thread

Silver cord

Sewing machine

Toy stuffing

Tassels

1 Copy the fish template on page 165 onto paper. Pin to the silk fabric and cut out a back and front section.

2 Position short lengths of ribbon across the width of the front section of the fish on the right side of the fabric. Sew the ribbon to the silk using appliqué stitch (see page 145).

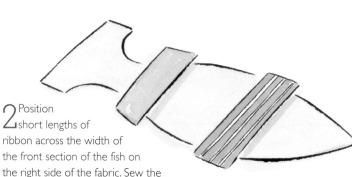

3 Place the front and back sections together with right sides facing. Loop a piece of silver cord and position it in the middle of the fish, sandwiched between the front and back sections, with the loop facing down inside. Pin and machine stitch around the edge leaving a gap of approx. 1½in. (4cm) in the seam.

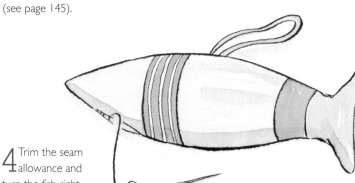

4 Trim the seam allowance and turn the fish right sides out. Stuff the fish until well shaped and firm. Sew up the gap, turning in the raw edges.

5 Decorate further by sewing on sparkly embellishments for the eyes and sequins for the scales. Finish by sewing a tassel centered on the underside of the fish.

Paper angel

It is traditional to place an angel or a star as the finishing touch on the top of a Christmas tree. Made from folded and cut white paper, this angel is elegant, sophisticated, and timeless. Carefully pack it away at the end of the holidays and you will get many years of pleasure from its simple grace.

materials

Large sheet of thick white drawing (cartridge) paper

Large sewing needle and matching cotton thread or embroidery floss (thread)

Double-sided tape or glue

Tracing paper

Pencil

Hole punch with ⅟₁₆in. (1mm) and ⅛ in. (3mm) heads

Decorative edged scissors

Craft knife

Cutting mat

Paperclip

1 Cut a piece of white paper measuring 26 × 10in. (66 × 25cm). Fold over a ¾in. (2cm) deep strip across the width of the paper. Turn the paper over and turn back another ¾in. (2cm) strip to make a pleated zig zag. Fold the strip again, turn the paper over, and repeat until you reach the end to create a concertina fold.

2 Thread a large needle with strong thread or embroidery floss. Push the needle and thread through all the pleats until you reach the end.

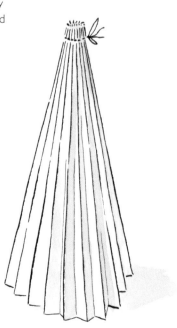

3 Gently pull the thread so that the two ends of the pleated paper meet to form a cone. Tie the thread with a couple of knots to secure.

4 Apply glue or double-sided tape down the length of the outer strip on one half. Stick this to the last strip on the other side of the pleated paper to complete the cone.

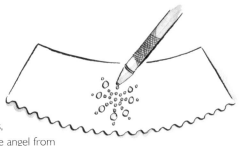

5 Copy the templates on page 154 and cut out the body, wings, and head of the angel from the white paper. Transfer the pattern from the template (see page 146) and position it centered on the front of the body. Use a hole punch with different-sized heads to punch out the design. Cut along the bottom edge with a pair of decorative edged scissors.

6 Bend the paper around and glue a ⅜-in. (1-cm) strip down one edge. Glue this to the other edge of the body to form a cone shape. The opening at the top should be approx. 1¼ in. (3cm) across.

7 Place a dab of glue on the inside of one short edge of the head and stick it to the opposite side to form a loop. Stick this to the inside of the front top edge of the body piece.

8 Use a hole punch to make the decorative edge along the wings. Stick the wings to the back of the body piece. Position the body piece over the pleated cone, using a few dabs of glue down the inside back join to secure it in place.

9 To make the pleated fan shape, cut a piece of paper 5¼ × 19¾ in. (13 × 50cm) and pleat it following the instructions in step 1. When you have finished pleating, use a craft knife to cut a triangle from the end of the strip and cut two more triangles, positioning them 1in. (2.5cm) and 2in. (5cm) from the top of the pleated paper.

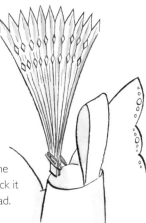

10 Use a paperclip to secure the end of the fan shape and tuck it in the body section behind the head.

Added sparkle

This project is a great one to do with children, who will probably enjoy embellishing the angel further with sparkly glitter, sequins, and even colorful overlays of tissue paper. You can also vary the size of the angel, making smaller ones to hang as tree decorations, suspended with a fine thread looped through the head.

Felt owls

Owls are perennially popular and no wonder—it is such a cute image that lends itself to all kinds of projects. Here I have used felt and embroidery to create these adorable little decorations. They look perfectly at home nestled in among the fir tree branches or perched on painted twigs.

1 Copy the owl templates and stitch markings on page 148 onto card (see page 146) and cut out. Draw around the card templates on felt and cut out.

materials

Tracing paper and pencil
Card
Felt in assorted colors
Matching sewing thread
Embroidery floss (thread) in assorted colors
Embroidery needle
Buttons or silver beads for eyes
Ribbon
Mini pom-pom trimming
Sewing machine
Toy stuffing

2 Sew the eye pieces, the two wings, and the beak to the front section of the body using appliqué stitch (see page 145) and matching thread.

3 Next, embroider the patterns on the eyes, body, and wings, following the markings on the template and using contrasting floss (thread) where desired. Sew on a silver bead or button for each eye.

4 To make the tassels, wind some embroidery floss (thread) around three fingers a few times. Slip the floss from your fingers and wind a length of floss around one end. Tie with a knot to secure. Trim the loops at the opposite end to make a tassel approx. 1½in. (4cm) long. Repeat to make a second tassel.

5 On the wrong side of the back section of the owl, position the tassels at the two points on the head, with the tassel ends facing upward. Center a loop of ribbon at the top and position two pom-poms centered at the bottom. Baste (tack) in place.

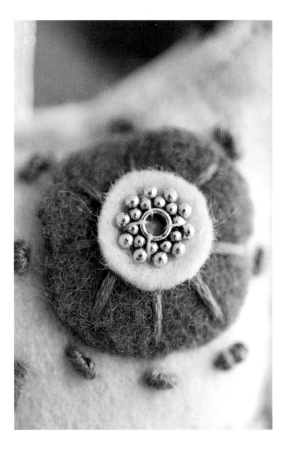

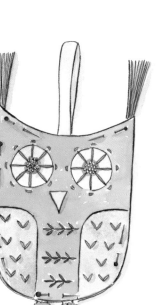

6 Position the front section of the owl over the back, with wrong sides together. Pin and machine stitch around the edge with matching thread, taking a seam allowance of ⅜in. (1cm) and leaving a gap of approx. 1½in. (4cm) for stuffing.

7 Stuff the owl until firm and well shaped, using the end of a paintbrush handle to push the stuffing into the ears. Sew up the gap with machine stitching to finish.

Curled paper star

One of the great things about working with paper is how a plain sheet can be transformed into something quite beautiful. These stars are made from strips of paper formed into heart shapes and curls that are stuck together to create this delicate sculpture. Hung against a white background, they cast wonderful shadows.

materials

Craft knife

Cutting mat

Pencil and rule

Several sheets of thick white drawing (cartridge) paper

PVA glue

Clothes pins (pegs) or small clips

1 Using a craft knife and cutting mat, and measuring accurately, cut the following from the paper: 12 strips 1¼ x 12in. (3.5 x 30cm); 12 strips 1¼ x 7in. (3.5 x 18cm); and 18 strips 1¼ x 11in. (3.5 x 28cm).

2 Take one of the 1¼ x 12-in. (3.5 x 30-cm) strips and bend it around to make a teardrop shape. Glue the ends together and hold in place with a clothes pin (peg) or clip. Repeat with the remaining 11 strips. Clip one strip to let the glue dry a little while you move on to the next strip.

3 Take two teardrop shapes and place a dab of glue approx. 4in. (10cm) up from the glued end. Glue one shape to the other and pin together as before. Make up six double teardrop shapes.

4 Glue the bottom two sections of the double teardrop shape together to form a heart shape.

5 Place the six pairs in a circle. Glue together where the curve of one pair meets the curve of the next pair.

6 Cut a piece of paper 1¼ x 2in. (3.5 x 5cm) and fold it in half. Add glue to the outer sides and push the folded paper down in the center where two pairs meet, gluing it to the base of each pair to secure. Repeat for each pair and clip each section together as it dries.

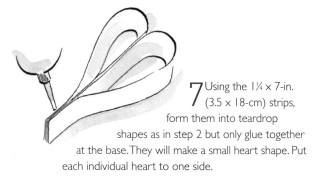

7 Using the 1¼ x 7-in. (3.5 x 18-cm) strips, form them into teardrop shapes as in step 2 but only glue together at the base. They will make a small heart shape. Put each individual heart to one side.

8 To make the curls, use the 1¼ x 11-in. (3.5 x 28-cm) strips and curl each strip around a pencil, stopping approx. 3in. (8cm) before the end of the strip.

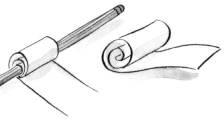

9 To assemble the star, glue the end of the small hearts made in step 7 and slot them into the center of the larger hearts that form the circle.

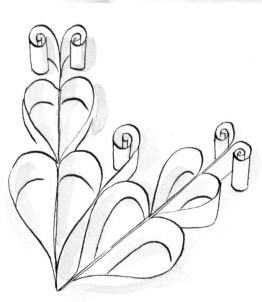

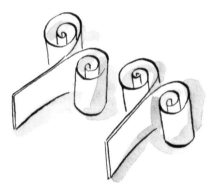

10 Take two curls made in step 8 and glue them together, with the curls facing in opposite directions.

11 Glue these into the center of the smaller hearts. Repeat for all six hearts.

12 Finally, slot the last six single curls in the gap between the two sets of larger hearts and glue in position.

Festive mice

Walnut shells are the perfect little bed for these cute mice. Decorate the shells with pretty Christmas ribbon or, for an extra bit of Christmas sparkle, paint them with gold or silver paint. Nestle them in the tree or find them resting places amongst the foliage along a mantelshelf.

materials

Tracing paper
Pencil
Scissors
Small scraps of felt
Sewing needle and matching thread
Toy stuffing
Small black beads
Walnut shells
Ribbon
Metallic paints and paintbrush (optional)

1 Copy the templates on page 146 onto card. Draw around the templates on felt and cut out the two side pieces, the base, the ears, and a strip for the tail from the felt. Using a small overstitch and matching thread, sew the two side pieces together from the nose to the tail end.

2 Poke the end of the tail into the back of the mouse at the center seam. Start at this point and pin the side parts to the base, easing the straight side pieces around the curved base. Sew in position using a small overstitch. Leave a gap of approx. ⅝in. (1.5cm) in the seam.

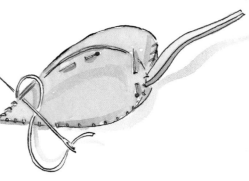

3 Push small pieces of stuffing into the mouse, using the end of a small paintbrush to push right into the pointed nose. When you have made a nice plump mouse, sew up the gap in the seam using overstitch.

4 Fold an ear in half at the base and sew in position on the side of the head approx. ½in. (13mm) up from the nose. Repeat for the other ear. Sew on small black beads for the eyes and nose.

5 Place the finished mouse in a walnut shell half. Decorate the shell with a little bow or paint it with metallic paint for a festive effect, if you like.

Ribbon tails

A fun way to display your mice would be to suspend them from the branches of the Christmas tree by their tails! Use a length of ribbon in place of the felt tail to make tying them on easier. Alternatively, line them up alongside children's place settings.

These cute little mice would also look fabulous in printed fabrics, mismatched for a patchwork effect.

Scandinavian horse garland

This pretty paper-cut garland is based on the little wooden painted dala horses of Sweden. On a white-and-silver themed Christmas tree, they will add some real Scandinavian charm. To complete the effect, make one to hang along the mantelshelf and add plenty of foliage for a natural look.

materials

Tracing paper
Pencil
Small scissors
Piece of white paper, 5½ x 12in. (14 x 30cm)
Glue

1 Copy the horse template on page 149 onto tracing paper and cut out the shape. Fold the piece of white paper in half. Position the tracing of the horse so that the nose is aligned with the fold of the paper. Using a pencil, lightly transfer the design onto the paper (see page 146).

Cutting out

You will need a steady hand and a sharp, small pair of scissors to cut out the design. Cut inside the lines you have drawn, so that they don't appear on the finished horse. You may find that a craft knife is also useful, especially for making the initial cut. If using a craft knife, always work on a cutting mat to avoid damaging your work surface.

2 Cut out the horse shape along the outline, carefully cutting through both sections of paper and not cutting the fold.

3 Fold the horse in half following the guide on the template. Don't press too firmly as you do not want the fold line to show. Cut out the patterns inside the lines, using a small pair of scissors. Repeat on the other folds and cut out the patterns for the legs and mane.

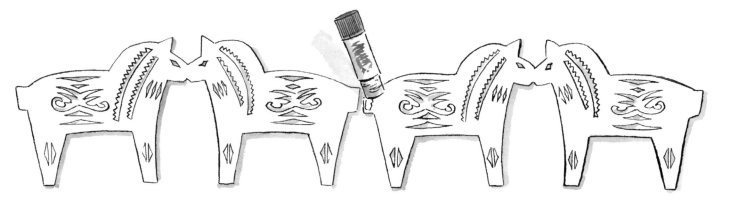

4 Open out the pair of horses. Repeat steps 1–3 to make more pairs and then join them together at the tail section with a dab of glue to make a garland of the required length.

Snowflake garland

Red-and-white decorations are always a stylish choice at Christmas. This simple Nordic-inspired garland, embroidered on felt and strung along a bright red cord or ribbon, will add a touch of Scandinavian charm to your mantelshelf or tree. Keep accessories simple and add some foliage for a look that is rustic but modern.

materials

Pencil

Scissors

Thick white felt for each star, approx. 4 × 4in. (10 ×10cm) each

Air-erasable pen or dressmaker's pencil

Dressmaker's carbon paper

2.2yd (2m) red cord, ribbon, or felt string

Red embroidery floss (thread)

Embroidery needle

Sewing needle and matching thread

1 Copy the star template and stitch pattern on page 155 onto paper and cut out the shape. Pin the template to the felt. Use an air-erasable pen to draw around the star shape and cut out. Cut as many stars as you want for your garland.

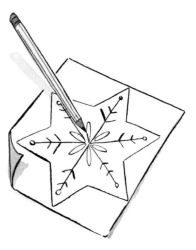

2 Put a sheet of dressmaker's carbon paper on top of the felt star shape, with the colored, carbon side face down. Place the star template on top. Draw over the design with a pencil to transfer the embroidery pattern onto the felt.

3 Using red or contrasting embroidery floss (thread) and following the stitch guide on the template, embroider the pattern on the felt star (see pages 144–145). This transforms the star into a pretty snowflake.

4 Position the finished stars along the length of cord at 15¾-in. (40-cm) intervals, sewing in place with matching thread. Make two loops in between each star and secure with a couple of stitches.

Embossed folk heart

Grouped together on the Christmas tree, hung along a mantelshelf, or tied on with red raffia to adorn a simple brown paper parcel, these pretty white hearts add a stylish look to your festive decorations. This is a great project for children, who will love rolling out and pressing different patterns into the clay.

materials

Tracing paper
Pencil
Scissors
Modeling clay
Rolling pin
Small knife
Implements with pointed ends to make patterns
White paint
Ribbon

1 Copy the heart template and patterns on page 147 onto tracing paper and cut out the heart shape. Roll out some modeling clay to approx. ¼in. (5mm) thick and 5in. (12cm) square.

2 Place the traced heart on the clay and cut around it with a small knife.

3 Use thin, pointed objects such as the tips of paintbrushes, knitting needles, or pens to mark out the pattern following the markings on the template. Use a small knife to cut out the inner shapes. If you feel unsure about copying the patterns by eye, lay the tracing paper heart on the clay heart and press down with a ballpoint pen over the pattern to mark it onto the clay.

4 Cut out small triangles all around the outside of the heart to give it a pretty, decorative edge. Make a large hole at the top of the heart for the ribbon tie.

5 Let dry and then give the heart a coat of white paint. Let dry. Finally, thread a length of ribbon through the hole and tie a bow to make a hanging loop.

Tin bird clips

I love making wreaths at Christmas. I like to have them inside and always make a very simple one out of entwined ivy sprigs to hang above the fireplace. Here, little silver tin birds attached to wooden clips sit perched among the foliage and berries. Make a whole flock and clip them to the tree, to gifts, to napkins, or place holders—the possibilities are endless!

1 To make the foil bird clips, copy the bird template and pattern on page 163 onto tracing paper and cut out the shape.

materials

Tracing paper

Pencil

Scissors

Small piece of aluminum foil from a disposable roasting tray

Old ballpoint pen

Strong double-sided tape or glue

Wooden clothes pins (pegs) or clips

FOR THE WREATH

Wire wreath base

Moss from a florist

Thin wire

Foliage

Silver leaves and decorations

2 Place the bird shape on a piece of foil and draw around it with a ballpoint pen—an old one that has run out of ink is ideal. Press firmly to indent the tin.

3 Cut out the bird shape. Take care, as the edges are sharp, and do not use your best fabric scissors as the blades will blunt very easily! Lay the traced template back on the foil bird and trace the patterns with the ballpoint pen, pressing firmly.

4 Attach the bird to the front of a wooden clothes pin (peg), using strong double-sided tape or glue. Repeat steps 1–4 to make as many birds as required.

5 To make the wreath, take some moss and start wrapping and pressing it around the wire wreath base. Use thin wire to secure it in place.

6 Place the foliage around the wreath by poking it into the moss and securing with wire. Add some silver leaves or strands of small silver decorations for a little sparkle. Clip the foil birds into position amongst the leaves and add a loop of wire to the back to hang.

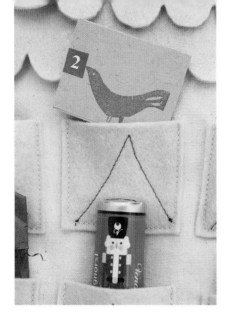

Advent calendar

Traditionally, advent calendars are made from card with little windows to open each day to reveal a picture. This charming advent calendar, in the shape of a house, can be used year after year and personalized to suit the age and preferences of its recipients. Fill the tiny pockets with hand-picked treats. It doesn't have to be much—a wrapped candy, a small charm or gift, a picture, or a note. This is all you need to make it a very special countdown to Christmas.

materials

Tracing paper or card

Pencil

Scissors

Piece of thick cotton or canvas, 17¼ x 25¼in. (44 x 64cm)

Piece of felt, approx. 12 x 17¾in. (30 x 45cm)

Sewing machine

Red cotton and matching sewing thread

Air-erasable pen

7in. (18cm) ribbon

1 To make the template for front and back section, copy the roof section from the template on page 161. Continue the dotted line to measure 25in. (64cm) from the point of the roof. Continue the line on the other side of the oblong until it is the same length. Join together with a line to make the base of the oblong. Fold the piece of canvas in half, lay the template with the dotted line along the fold. Cut out the house shape and then repeat to make two identical pieces. Use the template to cut out the door and 24 oblongs each measuring 2 x 1¾ in. (5 x 4.5cm), from the felt for the windows.

2 Transfer the drape (curtain) shape onto tracing paper. Cut the shape out and draw the drapes onto the 24 oblongs with an air-erasable pen. Machine stitch over the lines with red thread.

Make a date

To help keep track of the countdown you need to include the date, either on your wrapped gifts or attached to the pockets. Number stamps or stickers are perfect for adorning wrapped treats, or hand embroider numbers or stitch cut-out fabric numerals to each window. To keep the children guessing, place the numbered treats out of sequence.

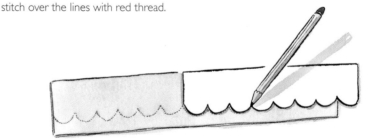

3 Copy the tile template on page 161 and transfer to tracing paper or card, then cut out. Draw around the template on the felt to make up four sections of roof tiles measuring 12½in. (32cm), 9½in. (24cm), 7in. (18cm), and 4¼in. (11cm) in length. Move the template along to get the required length.

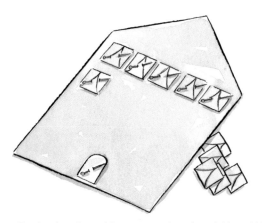

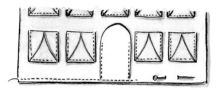

4 Pin the door in position, centered on the width and ½in. (13mm) up from the bottom edge. Next, position the windows in five rows. Start with the top row, positioning five windows so that their bottom edges are 10½in. (27cm) up from the bottom edge of the house. Leave a border of 1in. (2.5cm) on each side and space them out evenly. Pin in place. Position the other four rows evenly, finishing with the base of the last row of four windows, 1½in. (4cm) from the bottom edge.

5 Using matching thread, machine stitch around the two sides and base of each window to make a pocket. Keep the stitching close to the edge. Machine stitch the door, leaving the curve at the top unstitched to create a pocket.

6 Pin the longest section of tiles so that the top edge is 3in. (8cm) down from the roof top. Leave an equal overlap at each side and then machine sew in position with matching thread. Sew the remaining three sections of tiles, spacing them at ¾-in. (2-cm) intervals above each other. Trim the overlapping pieces of felt flush with the roof edge.

7 Pin the back and front house pieces together, with right sides facing. Fold the length of ribbon in half and tuck it inside at the top point of the roof, with the loop facing down inside. Leave the two ends sticking out and pin in place. Sew around the sides and roof, taking a ⅜-in. (1-cm) seam allowance, but leave the bottom edge open.

8 Turn right sides out. Fold under a ½-in. (13-mm) hem along the bottom edge, pin, and top stitch along the edge to finish.

Window paper cut scene

You often see paper cut snowflakes stuck to windows at Christmas, but this beautiful Polish-inspired woodland scene takes it one step further. It is much easier than it looks and the results, with a bit of careful cutting, are simply stunning. You don't have to stick it to a window—try mounting it on colored card and framing it for a special gift.

materials

Tracing paper
Pencil
Sheet of white drawing (cartridge) paper
Craft knife
Cutting mat

1 Copy the template on page 170 onto tracing paper. Take care to trace all the design clearly.

2 Cut out a piece of white paper measuring 13 x 11 in. (33 x 27.5cm). Fold it in half and lay the trace down on the fold line. Go over the trace with a hard pencil to transfer the pattern (see page 146).

3 Using a sharp craft knife, carefully cut out all the sections inside the lines, following the tinted areas on the template, through both layers of paper.

4 Gently unfold the paper to reveal the symmetrical image. Attach to a window with sticky tape.

Embroidered stockings

Hang out these beautifully embroidered stockings on Christmas Eve to make one of the best-loved Christmas traditions even more special. Make one for each member of the family—they are sure to be treasured for years to come. These instructions are for the Christmas tree design; for the other designs, follow the method below using the templates on pages 167 and 168.

materials (to make one stocking)

Piece of felt or boiled wool, approx. 21¼ x 23½ in. (54 x 60cm)
Piece of contrasting felt, 9½ x 6¾ in. (24 x 17cm)
Scissors
Dressmaker's carbon paper and pencil
Red embroidery floss (thread)
Cream embroidery floss (thread)
Embroidery needle
Needle and matching sewing thread
Sewing machine
Length of ribbon, 20½ in. (52cm)

1 Enlarge the stocking template on page 166 to the required size and cut out the front and back pieces from the felt or boiled wool. Copy the Christmas tree shape on page 169 and cut out from contrasting felt.

2 Put a sheet of dressmaker's carbon paper on top of the felt Christmas tree shape with the colored, carbon side face down. Place the tree template on top. Draw over the design with a pencil to transfer the embroidery pattern onto the felt.

3 Follow the stitch guide on the template and use doubled red embroidery floss (thread) to embroider the pattern (see pages 144–145). When making the bullion knots at the edge of the tree, note that they increase in size as they are worked along the branch. Make the smaller ones by winding the thread twice around the needle and the largest ones by winding the thread four times around the needle.

4 Sew the embroidered tree to the front of the stocking using appliqué stitch (see page 145), positioning it 4in. (10cm) down from the top edge and centered on the width.

5 Embroider the star and knots (see pages 144–145) around the tree in cream floss (thread), following the stitching guide on the template. Note that the bullion knots increase in size along the outside edge of the branch.

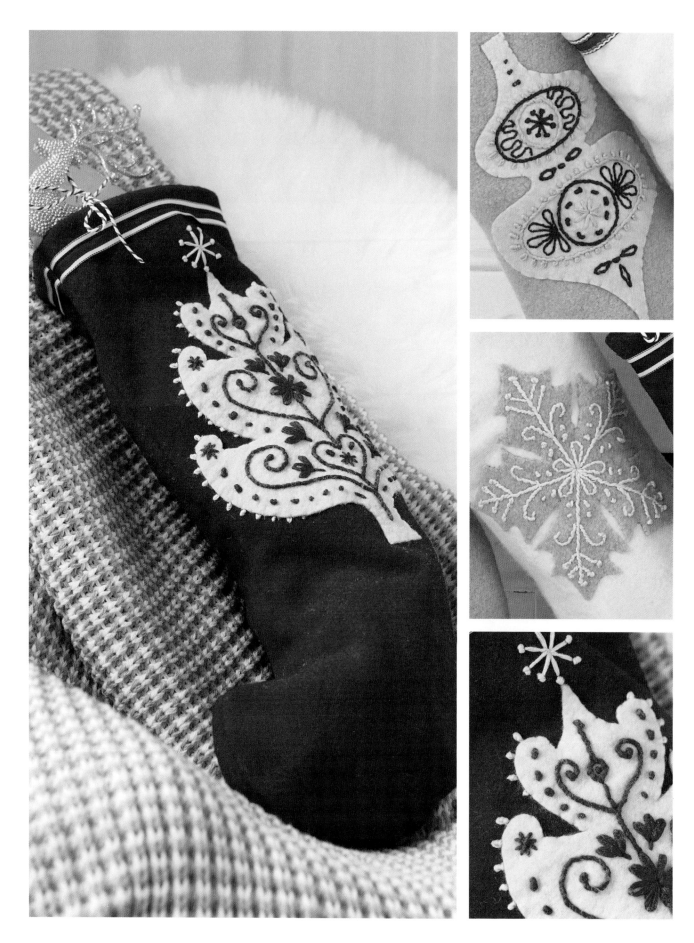

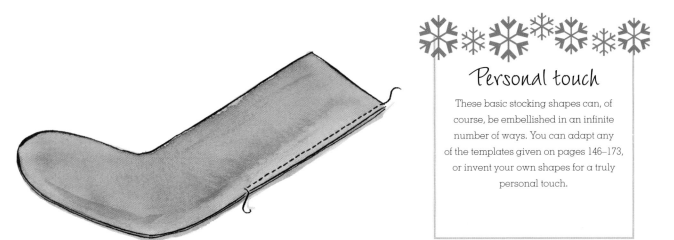

Personal touch

These basic stocking shapes can, of course, be embellished in an infinite number of ways. You can adapt any of the templates given on pages 146–173, or invent your own shapes for a truly personal touch.

6 Place the front and back sections of the stocking right sides together and machine stitch down the right edge to the heel, taking a ½-in. (13-mm) seam allowance.

7 Open the stocking out flat. Fold over a hem of approx. 1 in. (2.5cm) along the top edge. Pin the length of ribbon along the top edge approx. ⅜ in. (1cm) down. Machine stitch the ribbon to the middle seam on the front section. Sew a few rows of stitching across the width of the ribbon to strengthen it.

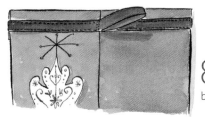

8 Fold a loop of ribbon at the center seam, then repeat the stitching to secure the ribbon on the back section.

9 With right sides together, sew approx. 2½ in. (6cm) of zig zag stitch on the top of the seams to strengthen. (If using a fabric that frays, zig zag stitch the edge of the seam all around the stocking.) Trim the seam allowance and clip the curved edges, then turn right sides out, and press to finish.

Quilled bird card clips

Pick out your favorite Christmas cards and make a special feature of them with a row of little bird card clips and string. Strung along a mantelshelf, they would make a charming display. Make a few extra to attach to gifts or clip them among the branches of the Christmas tree.

materials

Tracing paper
Pencil
Scissors
Sheet of white card
White quilling strips, ⅛ in. (3mm) wide (or wider if preferred)
Craft knife
Cutting mat
Quilling tool
PVA glue
Hole punch
Wooden clothes pins (pegs)
String

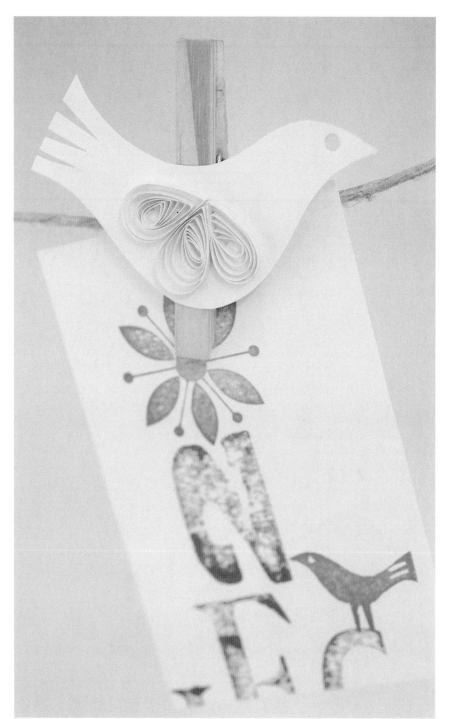

1 Copy the template on page 146 onto card and cut out the required number of bird shapes.

2 Cut a length of a quilling strip in half. Place the end in the split at the top of the quilling tool. Start winding the strip around the tip of the tool, keeping it tight.

3 When you have finished winding, release the strip of paper, so that it springs loose, and remove it gently from the quilling tool. Place a dab of glue at one end of the quilling paper and stick it down to make a closed circle of spiralled paper approx. ⅝in. (1.5cm) in diameter. You do not have to be exact, as it looks charming with slightly different-sized pieces.

4 With your finger and thumb, gently squeeze one side of the circle spiral together to form a teardrop shape. Repeat steps 2–4 to make a total of three teardrop shapes. Arrange as shown and glue in position on the bird.

5 Punch a hole in the bird shape to make an eye. Use a dab of glue to attach the finished bird shape to the clothes pin (peg). Clip onto a length of string and attach your cards to complete the display.

Pom-pom decorations

Pom-poms are enormous fun to make and a great way to introduce children to craft. These decorations have a homespun, folky appeal, but are brought bang up to date by using cool colors in cream, pale blue, and green. Pom-poms in bright colors also make a lovely addition to gift-wrapped presents.

materials

Cream wool yarn
Pencil
Scissors
Air-erasable pen or dressmaker's pencil
Scraps of felt
Cream embroidery floss (thread)
Embroidery needle
Pom-pom trimming in matching color
Felt balls in matching and contrasting colors
Sewing needle and matching thread

1 These instructions are for the heart-shaped decoration. To make the other shapes, use different combinations of pom-poms and felt pieces. Make some pom-poms using cream yarn by following the instructions on page 145. For the heart-shaped decoration, make a small pom-pom, approx. ¾ in. (2cm) in diameter or use pom-poms from a length of trimming.

2 Copy the heart template on page 163 and cut out two heart shapes from felt.

3 Use an air-erasable pen or a dressmaker's pencil to draw the embroidery design on one felt heart, following the guidelines on the template.

Garland fun
Pom-poms lend themselves to a variety of festive decorations and a great way to employ their soft shapes and varied sizes is on a garland. Make a batch of pom-poms in bright colors and attach them to a length of ribbon or braid to adorn a mantelshelf or doorway, or drape them around the tree.

4 Using embroidery
floss (thread),
embroider the design on one of
the hearts (see pages 144–145).

5 On the
other felt
heart, pin the
pom-pom trimming
to the inside of the heart,
all around the edge. Sew in
position with small stitches and matching thread.

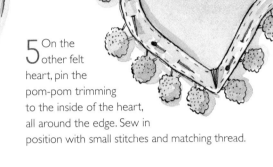

6 Thread a small pom-pom taken from
some trimming onto some embroidery
floss (thread) and thread on a felt ball. Take
a couple of small stitches (without going all
the way through the felt) across the heart with
the pom-pom trimmed edge. Bring the needle out
at the top of the heart.

7 Thread on some more
felt balls or homemade pom
-poms. Take the needle back
down through the last pom-pom
on the thread, leaving a loop to hang the
decoration. Secure the thread.

8 Place the
embroidered
heart shape on the back
heart shape, wrong sides
facing. Sew together with small
stitches all around the edge.

Rosette garland

This is a lovely project for using up leftover gift wrap. Use pretty bits of paper in a variety of colors for vintage appeal. These delicate rosettes are made from pleated fan circles—make them in different sizes, small ones to decorate gifts and giant ones for stunning hanging decorations.

1 To make the large rosettes, cut an oblong of gift wrap approx. 4 x 13½in. (10 x 34cm); for the small rosette, cut a piece of gift wrap measuring 2¼ x 6¾in. (5.5 x 17cm).

materials

Leftover gift wrap
Pencil and rule
Scissors
Short lengths of wire
Glue
Paperclips
String
Large needle

2 Place the large oblong on your work surface, pattern side down, and fold over a ⅜-in. (1-cm) strip across the width of the paper. For the smaller rosette, fold over approx. ¼in. (5mm).

3 Continue to fold over the strip, making a neat crease each time, then turn the paper over and fold back until you reach the end and all of the oblong is concertina pleated.

4 Fold the pleated strip in half and press firmly. Secure the fold with a short length of thin wire, wound around the crease and twisted to secure.

5 Open out the two halves and apply glue down the length of the outer strip on one half. Pull the pleated strip into a circle and stick the unglued outer strip to the glued half to complete the circle. Hold in place with a paperclip while the glue dries.

6 When you have made a few rosettes in the two sizes, thread a length of string onto a needle and thread the circles onto the string to make up the garland. Take a couple of stitches in the outer edge and alternate large rosettes with small ones.

Papier-mâché baubles

Papier mâché, from the French for "chewed paper," is an ancient craft that is still used all over the world from traditional folk artists to contemporary designers. To achieve the bauble shapes, I used polystyrene forms that you can buy from craft suppliers. This is a great project for getting the kids involved—they will enjoy the messy bits!

materials

2–3 sheets of scrap paper or newspaper
Bowl
PVA glue
Paintbrush
Polystyrene shapes in different sizes
White acrylic paint and paintbrush
Tracing paper
Soft and hard pencils
Acrylic paints in assorted colors
Silver fine liner pen
Varnish (optional)
Ribbon, ¼ in. (5mm) wide
Pin

1 Tear up your paper into small pieces approx. 1½ x 1¼ in. (4 x 3cm). Newspaper is ideal, but any thin paper will work.

2 The easiest way I have found to apply the paper to the shapes is to put some PVA glue in the bottom of a bowl. Thin it with a little water. Put some pieces of paper around the bowl and brush them well with the PVA. You can do a few at a time and it contains the mess a little!

Paper choice

To prevent any dark areas from showing through the paint, or colors bleeding, use scraps of paper that are lightly printed with text, avoiding those that include solid areas of color or printed pictures.

3 Start sticking the paper to the polystyrene shapes. You will only need a couple of layers. Place the covered shapes on a sheet of newspaper and let dry overnight. It may take a little longer depending on how many layers you have applied.

4 When dry, paint a base coat of white over the shape. If you have used newspaper, you may need a couple of coats to cover the print. Rest the bauble in a glass while you paint it, so that you can turn it around to cover all sides. Let dry. Once dry, touch up any marks left from the rim of the glass.

5 Copy the designs on page 160 onto tracing paper with a soft pencil. Attach the trace to the front of a bauble and go over the lines with a hard pencil to transfer the design (see page 146). Remove the tracing paper and redraw the lines with a pencil if necessary.

6 Use acrylic paints and a silver pen to paint in the designs. Once dry you can give the bauble a coat of varnish, if you wish.

7 To finish, fold an 8-in. (20-cm) length of thin ribbon in half. Turn over approx. ¼in. (5mm) at the ends and attach to the polystyrene with a pin. Your bauble is now ready to hang.

Basic baubles

If you can't get hold of polystyrene balls, you could use balloons. Don't blow them up to their full capacity—keep them quite small. Cover the balloons in the same way with the torn-up paper, leaving a small hole. When the papier mâché is dry, pop the balloon, remove it, and add a few pieces of torn paper brushed with PVA glue to cover the hole.

CHAPTER TWO

Cards and Gift Wrap

Fur-trimmed greetings cards

Homemade festive greetings cards are always a delight to receive and these simple designs are equally delightful to make. With just a few materials, you'll have produced a pile in no time. Little luggage label gift tags complement the cards perfectly and would look charming dangling from a plain brown paper parcel under the tree.

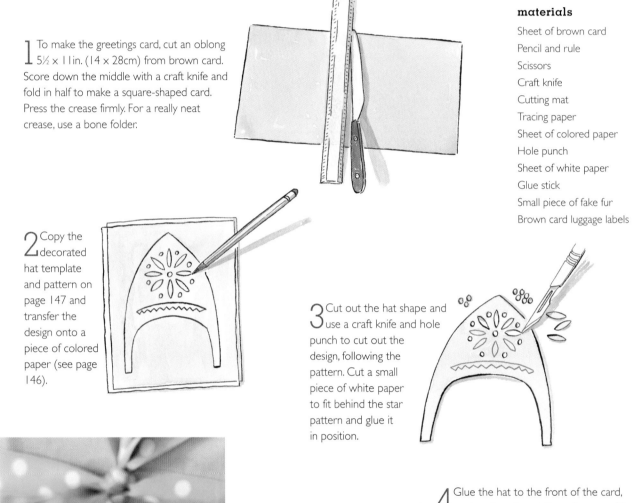

1 To make the greetings card, cut an oblong 5½ x 11in. (14 x 28cm) from brown card. Score down the middle with a craft knife and fold in half to make a square-shaped card. Press the crease firmly. For a really neat crease, use a bone folder.

materials

Sheet of brown card
Pencil and rule
Scissors
Craft knife
Cutting mat
Tracing paper
Sheet of colored paper
Hole punch
Sheet of white paper
Glue stick
Small piece of fake fur
Brown card luggage labels

2 Copy the decorated hat template and pattern on page 147 and transfer the design onto a piece of colored paper (see page 146).

3 Cut out the hat shape and use a craft knife and hole punch to cut out the design, following the pattern. Cut a small piece of white paper to fit behind the star pattern and glue it in position.

4 Glue the hat to the front of the card, centered on the width and approx. ¾in. (2cm) from the top edge. Stick some little pieces of fur to the earflaps and a small piece at the top for a bobble. If you wish, cut two small slits to represent the eyes.

5 To make the gift tags, follow steps 2–4, using the templates on page 147, and stick the shape to a brown luggage label. You can choose to leave the back of the design open, if you like.

Patchwork wrap and card

You can make wonderful original gift wrap out of scraps from the recycling box. I collect bits of paper throughout the year, such as old labels, bits of packaging, stamps and envelopes, paper bags, and old comics. You can personalize the wrap for individual members of your family or your friends, with photographs and their initials cut from magazines.

materials

Sheet of brown paper (or an old sheet of gift wrap)

Scraps of labels, stamps, envelopes, graph paper, etc.

Sheet of thin white card

Rule

Craft knife

Cutting mat

Scraps of plain brown and red paper

Hole punch

Tracing paper

Pencil

Glue

1 To make the gift wrap, first wrap your present in a layer of brown paper or a sheet of old gift wrap. Cut out lots of scraps of paper in different-sized oblongs and start sticking them on like patchwork to cover the base layer.

2 To make the greetings card, cut an oblong of white card measuring 6 x 12in. (15 x 30cm). Mark the halfway point on the top and bottom edges. Join these two marks, score, and then fold the card in half.

3 Cover the front of the card with scraps of envelopes and graph paper for the background. Copy the templates on page 146 and cut out the three sections of the bird. I used plain brown and red paper for the first two sections and a scrap from an envelope for the circle on the wing. Punch out a hole for the eye. Position the bird ⅜in. (1cm) in from the right edge and glue in place.

4 To make the mini envelope in the bird's mouth, cut out the envelope shape from the template on page 146. Fold in the two side flaps, glue them, and fold the back section of the envelope over so that the sides of the back section align with the glued flaps.

5 Fold over the top flap of the envelope, but don't stick this part down; you need to keep it open so that you can place a little Christmas message inside!

Rubber-stamped cards

Making your own rubber stamps is an easy way to create original cards and gift wrap. Once cut, they keep for ever. Put together a collection to make endless combinations of patterns and designs. Look out for ink pads in unusual colors—metallic bronzes and silvers are perfect for Christmas.

materials

Tracing paper

Pencil

White erasers, approx. 2 x ¾ in. (5 x 2cm)

Craft knife

Cutting mat

Sheet of thin white card

Sheets of thin white paper

Rubber stamping ink pads in assorted colors

Luggage labels

1 Copy the templates on page 163 onto tracing paper using a soft pencil. Place the trace on the eraser and transfer the pattern (see page 146). Go over the lines with a sharp pencil, to make them clearer.

2 Use a craft knife to cut away a horizontal slice of the background, leaving the pattern standing proud by approx. ⅛ in. (3mm). For the triangles, simply cut the whole triangle out, making sure you have sharp edges and points.

3 To make the card, fold a piece of card measuring 6¾ x 7½in. (17 x 19cm) in half. Load the reindeer body stamp with ink and print a reindeer approximately ⅝ in. (1.5cm) up from the bottom edge. Print the antlers in place. Use the triangle stamp to make a forest above the reindeer. Clean the stamps in warm water before changing colors. Print the larger triangle in a circle to make the sun.

4 To make gift labels and wrap, print up some luggage labels. Make rows of repeat patterns in different combinations on white paper or brown parcel paper. To make a reverse star shape, transfer the design onto an eraser. As you cut the spokes of the stars, angle the blade inward at a slant. Then cut from the other side of the spoke, sloping the blade toward the middle so that you cut out a "V" shape.

Goody bags and gingerbread labels

Homemade candies and cookies make great gifts, and what better way to present them than in these traditional brown paper bags decorated with stitched hearts and gingerbread man labels? Their simple old-fashioned charm is given a festive touch with red-and-white ribbons. My sewing machine has a choice of decorative stitches, but you could use a zig zag stitch for an equally pretty effect.

materials

Thick brown paper
Glue or double-sided tape
Decorative edged scissors
Tracing paper
Pencil
Thin brown card
Hole punch
Craft knife
Cutting mat
Sewing machine and red thread
Thin white card
String
Ribbon

1 To make a bag, cut an oblong 10 × 7½in. (25 × 19cm) from the brown paper. Fold a strip ⅜in. (1cm) wide along one side edge.

2 Fold the oblong in half and open out again. Cut a ⅜-in. (1-cm) strip from the bottom edge of the side that does not have the folded edge. Fold the bottom edge of the side with the folded edge in by ⅜in. (1cm).

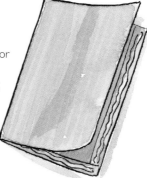

3 Place double-sided tape or apply glue to the two flaps. Fold the oblong in half, aligning the side and bottom edges. Press to seal the edges.

4 Use decorative edged scissors to cut a corrugated or patterned edge along the top of the bag.

5 To make the gingerbread labels, copy the templates on page 151 and cut out the shapes from thin brown card. Use a hole punch to cut out the eyes and make a hole to thread a tie through. Cut a mouth, using a craft knife.

6 Machine stitch a few lines of decorative stitching across the width of the gingerbread men and ladies. Thread a length of string through the hole to attach to gifts.

Cookie surprise

These goody bags are perfect for wrapping a matching gingerbread man cookie! Make a batch of gingerbread dough following the recipe on page 78, and cut out the gingerbread shapes using the card templates. Once cooled, pop them inside the bags and adorn with a matching label.

7 Follow steps 5–6 to make the heart labels from white card. You can punch a hole to thread a ribbon through or you can tuck the heart into a ribbon tied around the bag.

8 To make the oblong label, cut a piece of white paper 4¼ x 2½in. (11 x 6.5cm). Cut along one edge with decorative edged scissors. Sew a line of zig zag stitching ⅝in. (1.5cm) in from the decorative edge. Cut out the heart shape in the lower half of the label with a craft knife.

Button and paper flowers

These little decorative flowers have a charming vintage appeal. Attach them to gift wrap or wind them around napkins and finish with a vintage lace ribbon, tied in a bow. Look out for pearl buttons in thrift shops. You could try different types of buttons; small painted glass ones would be lovely. You can find the little bells at craft suppliers.

1 To make a button and bell flower, thread a bell onto a piece of wire approx. 8in. (20cm) in length. Fold the wire in half and thread a button on next, with the ends of the wire going through each of the buttonholes. Twist the wire around to secure beneath the button.

materials

Small silver bells
Thin wire
Wire cutters
Pearl buttons
Silver crepe paper
Glue

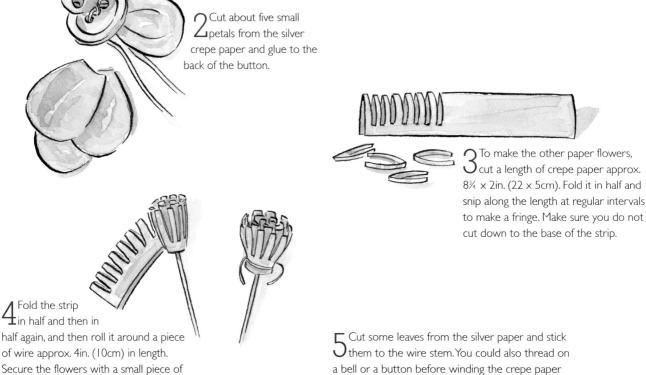

2 Cut about five small petals from the silver crepe paper and glue to the back of the button.

3 To make the other paper flowers, cut a length of crepe paper approx. 8¾ x 2in. (22 x 5cm). Fold it in half and snip along the length at regular intervals to make a fringe. Make sure you do not cut down to the base of the strip.

4 Fold the strip in half and then in half again, and then roll it around a piece of wire approx. 4in. (10cm) in length. Secure the flowers with a small piece of wire wound around the rolled paper.

5 Cut some leaves from the silver paper and stick them to the wire stem. You could also thread on a bell or a button before winding the crepe paper around, if you like.

Russian doll cards

I love to receive homemade Christmas cards. I really appreciate the care that has gone into them and always keep hold of them. These pretty sewn cards look very special, but are easy to make. Keep an eye out for colorful vintage buttons in thrift shops, as they make a good alternative to beads. You could make the dolls in different sizes by enlarging the template and sew them to a length of ribbon for a pretty folksy garland, too.

materials

Tracing paper
Pencil
Scissors
Small scraps of colored felt
Embroidery floss (thread) in assorted colors
Embroidery needle
Colorful bead or button
Pink fine liner pen
Sewing needle and matching thread
Card
Craft knife
Cutting mat

1 Copy the templates on page 171 and cut out the face and body from felt. Following the stitch guide, embroider the flower using daisy stitch (see page 144), centered on the lower section of the body piece. Embroider a French knot aligned with each petal (see page 145).

2 Sew a button or brightly colored bead to the center of the flower.

3 Following the stitch guide, embroider the face and draw some rosy cheeks with a fine liner pen. Sew the face onto the body using appliqué stitch (see page 145).

4 Cut a piece of card measuring 7½ × 3¾in. (19 × 9.5cm). Score down the middle and fold the card in half, pressing the fold down firmly. Glue the Russian doll in place, centering it within the square.

Cut-out bauble cards

These contemporary-styled greetings cards use bright metallic and sparkly card for a bold and vibrant look. The wonderful abstract shapes that are left over once you have cut out the baubles are stuck down on thin strips of white card to make stylish gift tags—they would look fantastic with silver gift wrap.

1 To make the tall card (Card A), copy the templates on page 158 and cut out the bauble shape and patterns from colored or metallic paper.

materials

Pencil

Scissors

Sheets of paper in bright and metallic colors

Sheets of thin white or colored card

Cutting mat

Craft knife

Glue

2 Cut a piece of colored card measuring 8¼ x 8¼ in. (21 x 21cm). Score down the middle and fold in half. For the other variations you will need pieces measuring: Card B 9½ x 4¾in. (24 x 12cm); Card C 8 x 6¼in. (20 x 16cm). For Card A, cut a piece of colored paper measuring 4¼ x 8¼in. (10.5 x 21cm) and stick it to the front of the card.

3 Stick the bauble shape on the card, centering the top edge of the bauble on the top edge of the card. Open the card and lay it flat on a cutting mat, right side up. Use a craft knife to cut around the right-hand edge of the bauble shape.

4 Following the template guide, glue the cut-out oval shapes in position and then glue the circles on top.

5 To make the gift tags, cut strips of thin white or colored card measuring 7 x 2¼in. (18 x 6cm). Glue a leftover shape onto the card.

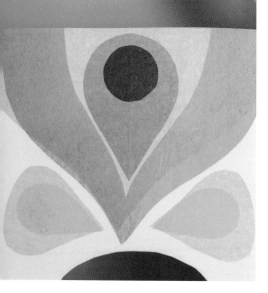

Layered tissue reindeer card

I love using layers of tissue paper in my designs. The overlapping colors make wonderful abstract shapes in rich and vibrant shades. You can follow the template or experiment with your own shapes. Don't worry about getting the tissue down in exactly the right position—you get beautiful and varied results if you position the tissue shapes in different ways.

materials

Tracing paper

Pencil

Scissors

Sheet of white drawing (cartridge) paper

Tissue paper in assorted colors

Craft spray adhesive

Sheet of colored card

Craft knife

Cutting mat

Metal rule

Bone folder (optional)

Glue

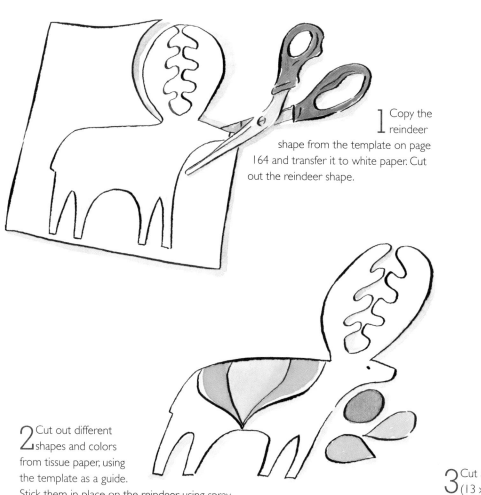

1 Copy the reindeer shape from the template on page 164 and transfer it to white paper. Cut out the reindeer shape.

2 Cut out different shapes and colors from tissue paper, using the template as a guide. Stick them in place on the reindeer using spray adhesive. Ensure your work space is well-ventilated and wear a mask. Alternatively, you can use a glue stick, but you need to take great care as the tissue paper tears easily.

3 Cut a piece of colored card 5 x 10¼ in. (13 x 26cm). Score down the middle and fold the card in half. Press the crease down firmly with a bone folder, if using.

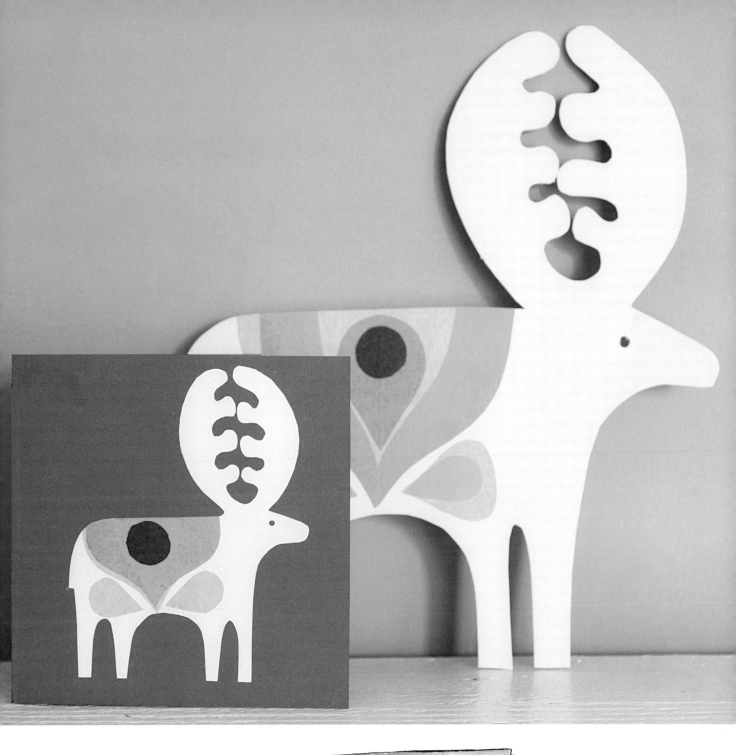

4 Stick the reindeer to the front of the card, centering it in the middle of the card. To make the large reindeer, follow steps 1–2 but enlarge the template by 50% and use thick card.

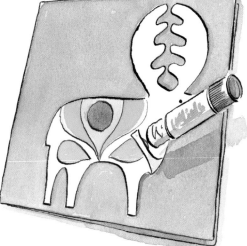

CHAPTER THREE

Cooking for Christmas

Iced snowflake cookies

There is a real homespun charm about edible things hung on the Christmas tree. Decorated with white icing and edible silver balls, these little ginger cookies are very pretty in a simple and elegant way. They're best eaten with a couple of days—that's if they last even that long!

1 Using a hand-held electric whisk, beat the butter and sugar together until soft and fluffy. In a separate bowl, beat together the eggs and syrup. Add them to the butter and sugar mixture and beat well to combine.

2 Sift the flour, baking powder, and ginger into the mixture and stir together until the mixture forms a dough. Gather it together into a ball. Cover and put in the refrigerator for 30 minutes.

3 Preheat the oven to 325°F (170°C/gas mark 3). Dust your work surface with flour and roll out the cookie dough to approx. ¼ in. (5mm) thick.

ingredients (makes 20)

GINGERBREAD DOUGH

Scant ½ cup (100g) salted butter

½ cup (100g) soft brown sugar

2 eggs

4 tsp light corn (golden) syrup

1 tsp baking powder

3 cups (300g) all-purpose (plain) flour

1 heaped tsp ground ginger

ICING

2 egg whites

2 tsp freshly squeezed lemon juice

2½ cups (330g) confectioner's (icing) sugar, sifted

Edible silver balls, to decorate

materials

Snowflake or Christmas-themed cookie cutters

Skewer

Nonstick baking sheets

Icing bag

Ribbon

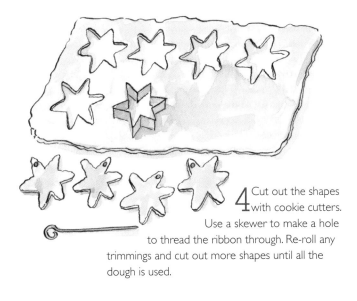

4 Cut out the shapes with cookie cutters. Use a skewer to make a hole to thread the ribbon through. Re-roll any trimmings and cut out more shapes until all the dough is used.

5 Put the cut-out shapes on nonstick baking sheets and bake in the preheated oven for 20 minutes or until golden. Transfer to a wire rack and let cool.

6 To make the icing, beat the egg whites with the lemon juice until combined. Add the sifted confectioner's (icing) sugar and beat on a low speed until the mixture is combined and smooth.

7 Spoon the icing into an icing bag and carefully decorate the cookies with a pretty pattern. Add silver balls before the icing sets.

Cookie heaven

Ginger and mixed spices are traditional Christmas flavors; however, you can easily adapt this recipe to make cookies in different flavors. For lemon cookies, add the grated zest of a lemon in place of the ground ginger. Or you could add a handful of chocolate chips or chopped nuts to the mixture instead.

8 To hang the cookies as decorations, thread a short length of ribbon through the hole. The cookies are best eaten as soon as possible, as they may soften in the open air. They will keep for 1–2 weeks in an airtight container.

Angel cupcake toppers

Cupcakes are lovely at any time of year, but these sparkly Christmas creations are very special. Using the same idea, you could make different toppers—little cut-out bells or stars would work well. It is best to keep the shape simple, as complicated shapes may be difficult to cut out. I have sprinkled some edible silver stars on my cupcakes for some extra festive glamour, but you could also use edible silver balls.

1 Copy the angel template and pattern on page 146 onto tracing paper and cut out.

materials

Tracing paper
Pencil
Scissors
Sheet of white paper
¼ in. (5mm) hole punch
Piece of silver card
Glue
Wooden toothpicks (cocktail sticks)
Sticky tape
Ribbon

2 Fold a small piece of paper approx. 2 x 2in. (5 x 5cm) in half. Place the angel template so that the straight edge aligns directly on the fold. Draw around the outline. With a pencil, lightly transfer the pattern onto the paper (see page 146).

3 Cut out the angel shape with a small pair of scissors. Keep the angel folded in half and carefully cut out inside the curved shapes.

4 Using the markings on the template as a guide, make a series of holes with a small hole punch.

5 Open up the angel and, using the markings as a guide, punch three holes along the top, middle, and bottom of the fold line.

6 Using a little glue, stick the angel shape onto a piece of silver card, then cut out around the edge of the angel. Attach a wooden toothpick to the back of the angel with a piece of sticky tape. Finally, tie a piece of ribbon in a bow under the angel.

Quince jelly

Quinces are a bit of a forgotten fruit. Inedible in their raw state, they are totally transformed when cooked into beautiful jewel-like amber and red preserves. They are highly aromatic, and a bowlful in your kitchen will give off a wonderful honeyed scent. You may be lucky enough to know someone with a quince tree in their garden, who would be happy for you to transform their fruit into something delectable in return for a jar of jelly.

ingredients

Quinces
Granulated sugar
Freshly squeezed juice of 2 lemons

materials

Jelly bag
Bowl
Preserve jars
Waxed (greaseproof) paper

1 Wash and roughly chop the quinces, there is no need to peel or core them. I have not specified a weight for the quinces, as it is the liquid produced from the fruit that you need to measure. Fill a saucepan with the chopped fruit and cover with water. Simmer gently until soft. Quinces are very hard, so this may take 2 or 3 hours! Add more water if the pan becomes dry.

2 Suspend your jelly bag over a bowl, without touching anything. The most popular method is to tie it to the legs of an upturned stool. Pour the fruit and liquid into the clean jelly bag and leave overnight to drip through.

3 Measure how much liquid you have collected in the bowl. Discard the bag and its contents. Place the liquid in a heavy-based saucepan and add 2½ cups (500g) of granulated sugar to 20fl oz. (600ml) of quince juice.

4 Add the lemon juice. Heat the juice and sugar gently, stirring every now and then until the sugar has dissolved. Bring the mixture slowly to a boil.

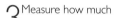

5 Continue to boil for 10 minutes and then test for set. Drizzle a little liquid onto a cold plate and let cool for a minute. Run your finger through the liquid: if it has reached setting point, the jelly should wrinkle up. If it does not, continue boiling and testing every 5 minutes until set.

6 When the jelly has reached setting point, pour the liquid into clean, warm sterilized preserve jars (see page 102). Cover with a waxed disc or a circle of waxed (greaseproof) paper and put the lid on. The lid should not be metal, but plastic-coated metal is suitable.

7 Cover the lid with patterned paper or fabric and tie with a ribbon. The unopened jelly will keep for up to a year. Once opened, store in the refrigerator and eat within one month.

Sugar mice

As a child, I always found a sugar mouse in my stocking. I still see them in the stores today and it brings back all the memories and excitement I felt on Christmas morning. Children love to help in the preparation for Christmas, especially in the kitchen, and this project is perfect. Wrapped in a piece of tissue paper and tied with a pretty ribbon, these little mice would make lovely gifts for their friends.

**ingredients
(makes approx. 12 mice)**

1 medium egg white
4 cups (500g) confectioner's (icing) sugar
1 licorice lace
Pink food coloring
String

1 Using a hand-held electric whisk, beat the egg white until frothy.

2 Sift the confectioner's (icing) sugar into the bowl and mix with a metal spoon to make a stiff mixture.

3 Divide the mixture in half and knead both parts into a ball. Add 2 or 3 drops of pink food coloring to one ball and knead until evenly distributed. Divide the two balls into approx. 12 similar-sized pieces.

4 Roll a piece into an oval. Flatten the base, make a pointed nose, and pinch out some ears.

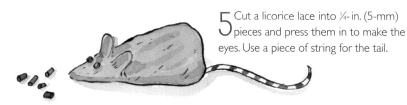

5 Cut a licorice lace into ¼-in. (5-mm) pieces and press them in to make the eyes. Use a piece of string for the tail.

6 Put the mice on a sheet of waxed (greaseproof) paper to dry for 24 hours. Store in an airtight container and eat within one week.

Cranberry and orange sauce

The Christmas meal would not be the same without cranberry sauce. The fresh taste of the berries with that extra bit of citrus burst goes perfectly with turkey. Serve it the following day (if there is any left over) with cold meat—it also makes a delicious addition to turkey sandwiches!

ingredients (serves approx. 12)

MY RECIPE USES DRIED CRANBERRIES. YOU CAN ALSO USE FRESH OR FROZEN, WHICH DO NOT NEED SOAKING, BUT YOU WILL NEED MORE SUGAR.

2¼ cups (350g) dried cranberries, or fresh or frozen

Grated rind (zest) of 1 orange

Juice of 2 oranges

Heaped 1½ tablespoons (20g) superfine (caster) sugar, or ¾ cup (150g) if using fresh or frozen cranberries

1 apple peeled, cored, and grated

1 cinnamon stick

1 Rinse the dried cranberries in hot water and then place in a saucepan with 3½ fl oz. (100ml) water. Simmer for 15 minutes. Remove from the heat and leave covered for about an hour, until the berries are nice and plump.

2 Add the remaining ingredients to the saucepan and return to the heat. Simmer gently for 10 minutes. If the sauce is getting too dry, add a little more water and orange juice.

3 Check for sweetness and add a little extra sugar if required. Let cool and remove the cinnamon stick before serving. Store in the refrigerator and eat within one week.

Gingerbread spires

Instead of the usual Hansel and Gretel-type gingerbread houses, I have based mine on Russian onion domes. With wonderful spires, turrets, and ornate decoration in gold and silver, they look as if they have appeared straight out of the pages of a fairy-tale book.

ingredients

1 quantity gingerbread dough (see page 78)
1 quantity icing (see page 78), divided into 4 separate bowls
Green, blue, and pink food coloring
Edible gold and silver balls

materials

Tracing paper
Pencil
Scissors
Sheet of white paper
Icing bag

1 Preheat the oven to 325°F (170°C/ gas mark 3). Follow steps 1–3 for the gingerbread cookie recipe on page 78 and roll out the dough. Copy the shapes for the domes from the templates on page 150 and cut them out from tracing paper. Put the shapes on the rolled out dough and cut carefully around with a knife.

2 Cut an oblong from paper measuring 4 x 1¾in. (10 x 4.5cm). Use this template to cut six oblongs out of the dough, following the instructions in step 1. You may need to re-roll the dough. Put the pieces on nonstick baking sheets and bake in the preheated oven for 20 minutes, until golden. Let cool.

3 Make one quantity of icing following the instructions in step 6 on page 81 and spoon into an icing bag. Squeeze some icing along the top edge of one oblong. Take another oblong, join the two top edges together, and stand them up so that they form a tent shape. The bases should not be more than 2in. (5cm) apart. Make up three tent shapes and put to one side.

4 Decorate the domes. Make up three batches of icing and color one batch pale green, one batch pale blue, and one batch pink.

5 Following the designs on the templates, decorate the domes using a combination of the colors. Don't worry if it is not perfect and looks different—you can make up your own patterns, too.

6 To add some sparkle to the spires, stick gold and silver balls into the icing before it sets.

7 Take one of the tent shapes and squeeze a line of icing up one long edge to the top of the triangle and then down the other side.

8 Stick one of the domes to the iced edge so that the triangle supports the dome and it can stand up. Repeat with the remaining two domes.

Interior decor

The domes and turrets are meant to be viewed from the front, but you can decorate the tent shapes too, if you like, so that you have a dazzling display from any angle. With all-over decoration, a cluster of spires, domes, and turrets would make a lovely centerpiece for the festive table.

Crystallized ginger

Ginger is a traditional spice to use in Christmas baking, but fresh ginger doesn't often appear on a festive menu. This lovely recipe will fill your house with a warm, spicy aroma. Serve these little treats after a meal with mint tea in Moroccan glasses, for an unusual alternative to coffee and chocolates.

ingredients

1 lb 2 oz. (500g) fresh root ginger
Superfine (caster) sugar

1 Peel and thinly slice the ginger. Put the ginger in a saucepan and cover with water. Cook for up to an hour, or until tender. Top up with water if the saucepan becomes dry. Drain.

2 Weigh the cooked ginger and measure an equal amount of sugar. Put the ginger back in the saucepan and add the sugar and 3 tablespoons of water.

3 Bring to a boil and cook until the liquid has almost evaporated. Stir frequently to prevent the ginger from sticking. Reduce the heat and continue stirring until almost dry.

4 Let cool and then toss the slices in sugar to coat. Store in an airtight container for up to three months.

Christmas chutney

A good chutney is an essential part of post-Christmas meals of cold cuts, cheese, and salads. This homemade version is made with dried fruit and is really quick to prepare and cook, even in the manic few weeks before Christmas. Dress the jar up with a hand-printed lid and label and you have a perfect festive gift.

1 Finely chop the onions and put in a preserving pan or a large heavy-based saucepan. Chop the dried fruit into small pieces and add to the pan.

2 Put all the remaining ingredients into the pan. Bring to simmering point and simmer for about 1¼ hours, until most of the excess liquid has evaporated. To check if it is ready, draw a wooden spoon across the top of the chutney to make a well. If the well fills with liquid then keep simmering and check again after 10 minutes. If before the hour is up the mixture becomes too dry, add a little more vinegar.

3 Prepare and sterilize the jars (see page 102). Spoon the chutney into the warm jars and place a circle of waxed (greaseproof) paper over the top of the chutney. Put the lid on. You can leave the chutney for 3–4 weeks to mature or you can enjoy it straight away! Once opened, keep in the refrigerator and eat within 3 weeks.

4 To make the paper cover, cut out a circle of white paper approx. 6in. (15cm) in diameter, using decorative edged scissors. Cut out two triangles from an eraser, load with ink from a stamp pad, and print the triangles in a circle to make star shapes.

5 Put the paper over the top of the jar, smooth it down over the sides, and secure with a length of ribbon. For the label, print the star pattern on a smaller circle of paper. Punch a hole and thread a tie or piece of string through to secure it to the jar.

ingredients
(makes 4 x 13-oz/370-g jars)

2 medium onions

2 cups (300g) dried ready-to-eat apricots

1 cup (150g) dried ready-to-eat mango

1 cup (150g) dried figs

1 cup (150g) dried dates

1 cup (150g) raisins

20fl oz. (600ml) cider vinegar

1 cup (200g) brown (muscovado) sugar

3 cloves of garlic, crushed

1 tbsp grated fresh ginger

1 tbsp ground coriander

1 tbsp mustard seeds

1 tsp ground allspice

1 tsp ground turmeric

2 tsp crushed dried red pepper flakes (chillies)

2 tsp salt

materials

Preserve jars

Waxed (greaseproof) paper

Sheet of white paper

Compass

Decorative edged scissors

White eraser

Ink pad

Ribbon or string

Hole punch

CHAPTER FOUR

Gifts

Flavored vinegars

Flavored vinegars make a lovely gift, as they are the kind of ingredient you tend not to buy for yourself. Simple to make, yet dressed up with a stylish label, they look very impressive. The zingy citrus taste will perk up any salad and will bring a welcome fresh taste to the festive table. Make a matching label for a bottle of olive oil and the lucky recipient will be ready to make a dressing in a dash!

1 To make the Lemon and Mint Vinegar, wash and crush the mint leaves slightly in your hand to bruise them and bring out the flavor. Put them in a sterilized jar (see page 102).

2 Use a zester or potato peeler to peel strips of lemon rind (zest). Take care not to include any of the white pith, which tastes bitter. Add the rind to the jar. Pour over the vinegar and replace the lid. Tip the bottle upside down each day for a week.

3 After a week, strain off the leaves and rind (zest) into a pitcher (jug) and then pour the vinegar into the sterilized bottles.

4 To make the Orange and Rosemary Vinegar, follow steps 1–3 but replace the lemon and mint with rosemary and orange rind (zest).

5 For a finishing touch, add a curl of lemon rind (zest) and a sprig of mint (or orange rind and a rosemary sprig) to the bottle before sealing. A piece of decorated tissue paper or gift wrap makes a simple wrap with a matching label. The unopened vinegar will keep for up to three months in a cabinet and should be used within one month after opening, and stored in the refrigerator.

ingredients

LEMON AND MINT VINEGAR
(MAKES TWO 9FL OZ./250ML BOTTLES)

A handful of fresh mint leaves, plus extra sprigs to decorate

17fl oz (500ml) white wine vinegar

1 unwaxed lemon

ORANGE AND ROSEMARY VINEGAR
(MAKES TWO 9FL OZ./250ML BOTTLES)

17fl oz (500ml) cider vinegar

1 orange

3 large sprigs of fresh rosemary, plus extra to decorate

materials

Large preserve jar with a lid

2 x 9fl oz. (250ml) bottles with lids

Zester or potato peeler

Sieve

Pitcher (jug)

Tissue paper or gift wrap, to decorate (optional)

Vanilla sugar

Homemade gifts are always welcome and this one couldn't be easier. Vanilla sugar is simply superfine (caster) sugar that has been infused with a vanilla pod. Add a spoonful to hot chocolate or use in baking recipes. Sprinkle over peaches and other fruit and roast in the oven for a simple and beautifully aromatic dessert. This is the type of store cupboard ingredient that no kitchen should be without.

materials

FOR THE VANILLA SUGAR
Glass preserve jar
Sharp knife
Vanilla pod
Superfine (caster) sugar

FOR THE LABEL
Tracing paper
Pencil
Sheet of thin white card
Craft knife
Cutting mat
Silver thread
Ribbon

1 To sterilize glass jars, first wash the jars in warm, soapy water. Place them in a saucepan of boiling water for 10 minutes. Remove and turn the jars upside down on a baking sheet and place in a hot oven to dry. You can also use a microwave oven: half fill the jars with cold water and heat them on high for approx. 3 minutes. The water must boil in the jars. Place them in the oven to dry.

2 Use a small, sharp knife to split open the vanilla pod and place it in a jar a quarter filled with superfine (caster) sugar. Top up with more sugar, place the lid on, and store in a dark, dry cabinet. You can top up the jar with more sugar as you use it. Replace the vanilla pod after a year.

3 To make the label, copy the template on page 164 onto thin white card. Use a craft knife to carefully cut out the shape and the pattern.

4 Write your message, or a recipe, on the label and thread a short length of silver thread through to tie it to the jar. Finish with a pretty ribbon to present it as a gift.

Gift-wrapped soap

It is lovely to give and receive presents, but they don't have to be expensive to be appreciated. With a little creative flair something small, such as a plain bar of soap, can become a gorgeous gift. Wrap a few and put them aside for unexpected visitors over the festive season. Try these gift-wrapping ideas on other gifts, too.

materials

Bars of soap

Scraps of pretty, patterned wallpaper

Sheets of plain colored paper or tissue paper

Scraps of origami or washi paper

Sheet of translucent paper

Double-sided tape

Glue

Sprigs of fresh or dried berries, eucalyptus, mini pine cones

Silver thread and silver ribbon

Red embroidery floss (thread)

Buttons or charms

1 To use wallpaper, take a scrap of patterned wallpaper and fold it around the soap. Secure with sticky tape. Make a tiny posy from sprigs of berries, eucalyptus, or mini pine cones and tie together with a sparkly silver ribbon. Attach it to the wrapped soap with double-sided tape.

2 For a brightly colored version, wrap the soap in a richly colored paper as a base. Cut a strip of origami paper and wrap it around the middle of the soap, securing with a dab of glue. Thread a button onto a length of red embroidery floss (thread). Wrap the floss twice around the strip of origami paper and secure with a looped knot.

3 For a sophisticated look, wrap the soap in a piece of translucent paper. Wrap some silver thread around the soap a few times, attach a charm, and tie a bow to finish. Try pearl buttons or pair up velvet ribbon with a vintage buckle for a really glamorous gift.

Little mice

If you decide to make this gorgeous pair of mice as gifts, you may have trouble parting with them! If you do manage to give them away, you know they will be well loved for years to come. You can use scraps of material for the bodies, but when using felt for the clothes try to find the best quality possible; it makes all the difference!

1 Make card templates for the different sections of the mouse, using the templates on page 172. Use the templates to cut out the required number of pieces from the linen, spotty, and contrasting fabrics.

materials (to make one mouse)

Paper or card for templates

Piece of linen, approx. 12 × 24in. (30 × 60cm)

Small scrap of spotty cotton

Small scrap of contrasting fabric for socks and scarf (I used a soft brushed cotton)

Sewing machine

Matching thread

Toy stuffing

Embroidery floss (thread) in two colors for eyes and nose

Embroidery needle

Piece of felt, approx. 12 × 9½in. (30 × 24cm)

Tiny buttons

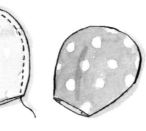

2 To make the ears, pin a piece of spotty fabric and linen together with right sides facing. Sew together, taking a ⅜-in. (1-cm) seam allowance, and leaving the straight edge open. Trim the seam allowance and clip the curves, then turn right sides out. Press. Repeat for the other ear.

3 To make the tail, cut a piece of linen measuring ¾ × 9¾in. (2 × 22cm). Fold in half and press. Turn the two ends in and the two long sides to the middle seam and then fold in half again. All raw edges will now be hidden. Pin along the length and machine stitch together, stitching close to the edge.

4 With right sides together, pin the sock section to the leg section along the short edge. Sew together, taking a ⅜-in. (1-cm) seam allowance. Trim the seam allowance and press the seam open. Repeat with the other leg sections, back and front.

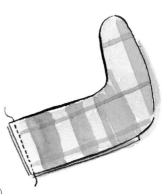

5 With right sides together, pin the leg sections together and machine stitch around the edges, leaving the top of the leg open and taking a ⅜-in. (1-cm) seam allowance. Trim the seam allowance and turn right sides out. Repeat with the other leg and the two linen arms.

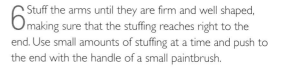

6 Stuff the arms until they are firm and well shaped, making sure that the stuffing reaches right to the end. Use small amounts of stuffing at a time and push to the end with the handle of a small paintbrush.

7 To assemble the body, fold the bottom of the ears in as shown and place both, spotty side facing out, on the right side of the head on one body piece, facing down the length of the body with the base of the ears sticking out over the top of the head by approx. ⁵⁄₁₆ in. (8mm). Place the arms facing into the body in the same way, positioning them at the shoulder. Baste (tack) to secure.

Winter wardrobe

If time allows, why not make a collection of small outfits for the mice? Using assorted colors of felt, you can make a variety of dresses or shorts and tops; alternatively, mix and match printed cotton fabrics to give the mice a spring wardrobe for the warmer weather!

8 Pin the front section of the mouse body to the back section, right sides facing. Sew together, taking a ⅜-in. (1-cm) seam allowance and catching the ears and arms in the seam. Trim the seam allowance and turn right sides out.

9 Stuff the head and body. Turn under a ½in. (13-mm) hem at the base of the body and position the two stuffed legs in between the front and back sections. Make sure both feet are facing toward the left. Pin and top stitch along the seam.

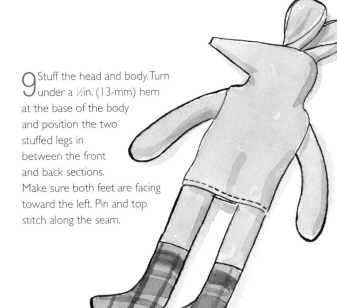

10 Sew two bullion knots for the eyes, a backstitch smile, and a satin stitch nose (see pages 144 and 145). Sew the tail on, positioning it on the lower back.

11 Use the templates on page 173 to cut out the clothes from felt. These are simply top stitched together at the seams. Sew on some buttons to the front of the dress or t-shirt, and cut a slit on the back as shown on the template, to help dress the mouse.

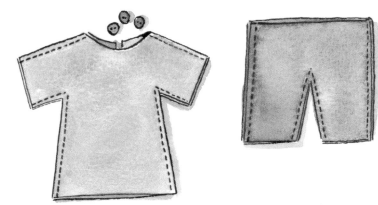

12 To make the scarf, cut a strip of fabric measuring 2¾ x 15¾in. (7 x 40cm). Fold in half with right sides together. Sew around the two ends and the long side, leaving a gap of 1⅝in. (4cm) for turning through. Trim the seam allowance, turn right sides out, slip stitch the gap closed. Press.

Winter throw

Draped over a sofa or folded over a chair, throws can change the look of a room and add interest to plain upholstery—they are also warm and cozy! The embroidery looks complicated but the stitch is very easy and one I use all the time to great effect. The design has a lovely folk appeal, but would sit quite happily in a contemporary setting.

materials

Tracing paper

Pencil

Scissors

Soft woolen fabric (not fleece), 40 × 60in. (100 × 150cm)

Dressmaker's carbon paper

Sportweight (4-ply) knitting cotton yarn in two contrasting colors

Embroidery needle

Felted fabric, 8 × 13¾in. (20 × 35cm)

Air-erasable pen

Sewing needle and matching thread

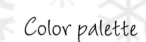

1 Copy the shape and design from the template on page 156. Place a sheet of dressmaker's carbon paper on one end of the woolen fabric throw with the colored, carbon side down, centering it 7in. (18cm) up from the short edge. Place the trace on top and go over it with a pencil to transfer the design to the fabric.

2 Embroider the circular design in whipped backstitch and bullion knots, following the marked pattern and using two contrasting yarns (see pages 144–145).

Color palette

I have chosen to use a subtle wintry palette of cream, gray, and black but the design would also look stunning in bright colors. Try combining bright pink and orange with touches of lime green for a totally different look.

3 Trace one scallop shape onto tracing paper and cut it out. Draw around the template with an air-erasable pen to make ten scallop shapes from the felted fabric.

4 Pin the scallop pieces around the edge of the embroidered circle. Sew in position using appliqué stitch and matching thread (see page 145).

5 Place a sheet of dressmaker's carbon paper over the embroidered circle and mark out the loop design around the scallop edge. Embroider the loop design using whipped backstitch (see page 144).

6 Following the method in step 1, mark out the two smaller flower designs (see page 156) so that the center of the flower is 4¼in. (11cm) from the scalloped edge on either side, roughly aligned with the central flower in the embroidered circle. Embroider the two flowers.

7 Embroider a bullion knot between each petal of the two small flowers and between each scallop, in contrasting yarns.

8 Turn over a double hem of ⅜in. (1cm) on all sides and pin in place. Use a contrasting color yarn to blanket stitch all around (see page 145).

9 Cut out three circles of felt, one measuring 7in. (18cm) in diameter and two measuring 2¼in. (5.5cm) in diameter. Pin the circles to the back of the throw to cover the stitches. Use small appliqué stitches (see page 145) to sew the circles in place, making sure that the stitches do not go through to the top of the fabric.

Vintage teacup candles

I love vintage china and can never resist a thrift shop or flea market to see what treasure I may find. I like to use them for storing needles and pins and jewelry, some make lovely displays, and I do drink tea from some of them! They can also be easily transformed into pretty candles that make lovely gifts or, when grouped together amongst the decorations, a charming display. Mix and match colors and patterns for a true vintage look.

materials (to make 4–5 candles)

Weighted wicks

Lollipop sticks or similar

Trivet (optional)

Large saucepan and smaller old saucepan that fits inside

17oz. (500g) wax pellets

Teacups and saucers

1 Place a wick in the bottom of the teacup. Tie the wick to a lollipop stick or something similar, such as a pencil, and lay it across the rim of the teacup. Make sure that the wick is centered in the cup and is pulled taut with the weight on the bottom of the cup.

2 Put a trivet, if using, in the bottom of the larger saucepan and add some water to the saucepan to approx. one third full.

3 Pour the wax pellets into the smaller saucepan and place it inside the larger one. Warm over a low heat while the wax melts slowly—do not stir. Never leave the wax unattended and watch that the water level does not get too low.

4 To prevent the cups from cracking, place them in a low oven to warm slightly. When the wax has become molten, pour it into the warmed cups, to approx. ¼in. (5mm) from the top. As the wax cools it will contract slightly and leave a dip around the wick. Melt any leftover wax to top up the candles. Let set.

5 Untie the lollipop stick and trim the wick to approx. ⅜in. (1cm). Place the teacup on a saucer if you wish.

Fur-lined baby boots

These cozy little boots are easy to sew and would make a lovely gift for tiny feet. I have made them with faux sheepskin, but you could also make them from felt lined with fleece. For an alternative embroidery pattern, try using one of the designs from the snowflake garland on page 155.

materials

Tracing paper
Pencil
Scissors
Thin card
Piece of faux sheepskin, approx. 15¾ × 23¾in. (40 × 60cm)
Air-erasable pen or dressmaker's pencil
Embroidery floss (thread) in contrasting color
Embroidery needle
Sewing machine

1 Copy the templates and patterns on page 159 for the sole, upper, and side sections onto tracing paper and make card templates.

2 Pin the templates to the fabric and draw around the shapes. Cut out the pieces. Make sure that the left and right side sections of the boots are cut with the fur on the inside.

3 Following the guide on the template, draw the embroidery design on the front section of the boot with an air-erasable pen, centering the design and positioning it ⅝in. (1.5cm) in from the toe. Embroider the star shape using straight stitch and bullion knots (see page 145).

4 Pin the two side pieces with wrong sides (fur sides) together, at either end. Machine stitch together taking a ⅜-in. (1-cm) seam allowance.

5 Pin the sole to the side sections. Start at the front toe section, centering this part first, and then gently ease the sole around to fit, pinning as you go. Baste (tack) in position.

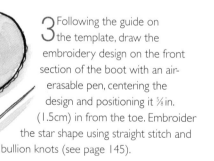

6 Using evenly spaced diagonal stitches and embroidery floss (thread), sew around the base to join the sole and side sections.

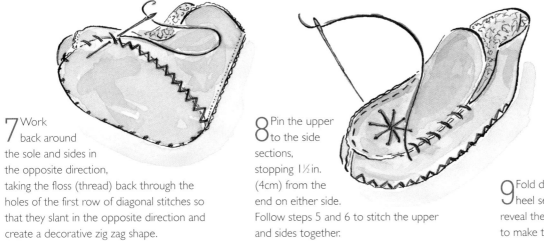

7 Work back around the sole and sides in the opposite direction, taking the floss (thread) back through the holes of the first row of diagonal stitches so that they slant in the opposite direction and create a decorative zig zag shape.

8 Pin the upper to the side sections, stopping 1½in. (4cm) from the end on either side. Follow steps 5 and 6 to stitch the upper and sides together.

9 Fold down the front flap and heel section of the boot to reveal the fur. Repeat steps 2–8 to make the second boot.

Polar bear hot water bottle cover

A cozy, covered hot water bottle makes a lovely Christmas gift, ideal for snuggling up with on the sofa watching all those old films shown over the holidays. If your hot water bottle is a different size, make up a new template by drawing around the bottle, adding 1-in. (2.5-cm) seam allowance to the sides and base and an extra 1½in. (4cm) at the top to turn down.

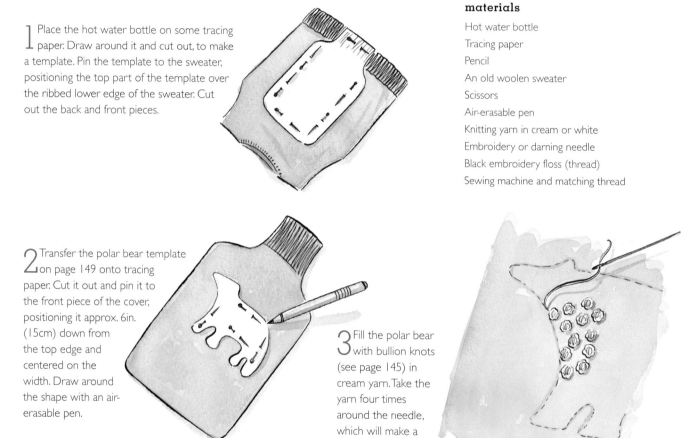

1 Place the hot water bottle on some tracing paper. Draw around it and cut out, to make a template. Pin the template to the sweater, positioning the top part of the template over the ribbed lower edge of the sweater. Cut out the back and front pieces.

materials

Hot water bottle
Tracing paper
Pencil
An old woolen sweater
Scissors
Air-erasable pen
Knitting yarn in cream or white
Embroidery or darning needle
Black embroidery floss (thread)
Sewing machine and matching thread

2 Transfer the polar bear template on page 149 onto tracing paper. Cut it out and pin it to the front piece of the cover, positioning it approx. 6in. (15cm) down from the top edge and centered on the width. Draw around the shape with an air-erasable pen.

3 Fill the polar bear with bullion knots (see page 145) in cream yarn. Take the yarn four times around the needle, which will make a nice rounded knot and a lovely textured surface for your polar bear.

4 Use black embroidery floss (thread) to make a bullion knot for the eye and add a few satin stitches for the nose.

5 Pin the back and front pieces together with wrong sides facing, just at the top ribbed section. Machine sew a zig zag stitch 1½in. (4cm) down each seam.

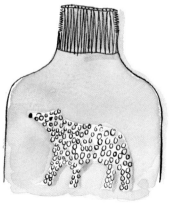

6 Turn the front and back inside out so that the right sides are together. Using zig zag stitch, sew down the sides and along the bottom edge, taking a ⅜-in. (1-cm) seam allowance. Trim any seam allowance, clip the curves, and turn right sides out.

7 Make a couple of pom-poms using the cream yarn (see page 145), approx. 1¾ in. (4.5cm) in diameter. Leave 5in. (12cm) of yarn attached to sew to the cover. Attach them to the side seam 1½ in. (4cm) down at the base of the first section of zig zag. Fold the hot water bottle in half to insert it into the cover and fold over the cuff by 1½ in. (4cm) to finish.

Felting

Before cutting out, you could felt the sweater by placing it in a very hot cycle in the washing machine but remember that the jumper will shrink, so make sure it will provide enough fabric for the front and back.

Embroidered dala horse

Dala horses are traditional Swedish carved and painted wooden toys that were originally made during the long, dark winter evenings for children. They are still handcrafted today and have become a national symbol of Sweden. I have created a little soft version of the horse, hand-embroidered with cheerful, brightly colored yarns.

materials

Tracing paper
Pencil
Paper
Air-erasable pen
Scissors
Soft fabric, approx. 10 x 23½in. (25 x 60cm)
Small scraps of felt in assorted colors
Tapestry yarns or small scraps of knitting yarn
Dressmaker's carbon paper
Large embroidery needle
Sewing needle and matching thread
Toy stuffing
Sewing machine and matching thread

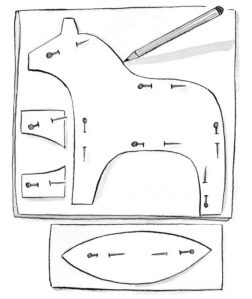

1 Copy the templates on page 171 onto paper and cut out. Fold the main fabric in half, pin the horse's body pieces to the fabric and draw around each piece with an air-erasable pen. Cut two pieces for the front, back, and leg pieces. Cut one underbelly piece.

2 Draw around the templates for the embroidered pieces on the scraps of felt and cut out. Put a sheet of dressmaker's carbon paper with the colored, carbon side down over each piece, with the traced pattern on top, and transfer the embroidery pattern onto the felt. Embroider the pattern following the stitch guide (see page 171).

3 Following the template guide, pin the felt pieces in position on the front section. Use appliqué stitch (see page 145) and matching thread to sew in place. Transfer the stitch guide for the reins using carbon paper. Embroider the reins and add bullion knots around the appliquéd pieces, as marked on the template.

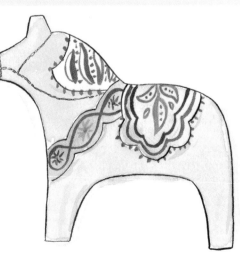

4 With right sides together, pin and machine stitch the inner legs to the two body pieces along the side and bottom edges, taking a ½-in. (13-mm) seam allowance.

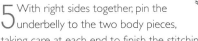

5 With right sides together, pin the underbelly to the two body pieces, taking care at each end to finish the stitching at the point. Baste (tack) and machine stitch, leaving a 2-in. (5-cm) gap in the seam at the top of one of the legs to turn the horse the right way out.

6 Starting where the inner legs join the body, pin and machine stitch the front and back together, taking a ½-in. (13-mm) seam allowance. Match up the line of stitching on the legs and continue around the body.

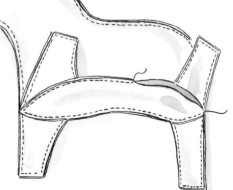

7 Trim the seam allowance and clip the corners of the legs. Turn the horse the right way out through the gap. Use the handle of a thin paintbrush to ease the nose and ear into shape.

8 Stuff the horse, using the paintbrush handle to push the stuffing down into the ears, nose, and legs. Use small pieces of stuffing and continue until the horse is firm and well shaped. Keep the stuffing firm at the top of the legs. Turn under the raw edges in the front leg seam, pin, and slip stitch the gap closed.

Color schemes

Red is a traditional color for the Swedish dala horses, and would look suitably festive as an alternative to the lovely bright yellow used here. However, the wooden horses are now made in many colors and you can adapt your scheme to suit what you have available in your scrap basket—combined with colorful embroidery floss (thread) and cheerful felts, the effect will be as charming as the originals.

CHAPTER FIVE

Table Decorations

Robin place names

Place names add a sense of occasion to the Christmas table. Your family and friends will appreciate the care you have put into the table setting and little personal touches like these cute robins make all the difference. Add some fresh green foliage and some silver twigs to complete the look.

materials (to make 6 robins)

Tracing paper and pencil
Sheet of brown card
Small sheet of white paper
Small sheet of red paper
Craft knife
Cutting mat
Small scissors
Decorative edged scissors
Glue
¼in. (5mm) hole punch
Paintbrush
White or silver paint
6 pine cones

1 Copy the templates on page 155 and transfer the robin to brown card, and the leaf and wing to white paper. Cut six of each. Also cut six circles, 1¼in. (3cm) in diameter, from red paper.

2 Fold a red circle in half and in half again. Transfer the pattern from the template on page 154. Using a small pair of scissors, cut out the small triangles along each folded side as if you were making a paper snowflake. Cut a decorative edge with shaped craft scissors or by hand, and unfold.

3 Glue the wing and red breast in position on the robin's body. Punch a hole for the eye with a hole punch. Glue the leaf in position behind the beak. Repeat steps 2–3 for the remaining robins.

Pen to paper

You can either write your guest's name on the leaf before or after you stick it in place. Choose a pen with metallic ink, if you wish, to complement the painted pine cone.

4 Add a little white or silver paint to each pine cone. Let dry. Push the robin's legs into the pine cone and move the robin around until the pine cone balances and the robin is safely perched.

Scandinavian tea light lanterns

Lighting candles at the Christmas dinner table always adds to the festive occasion. You can make it even more magical with these lanterns in the shape of pretty Scandinavian houses and decorative fir trees. The light will shine through the miniature windows and heart shapes, creating a lovely warm and welcoming setting for your guests.

materials

Pencil

Scissors

Sheets of thin white card or thick drawing (cartridge) paper

Craft knife

Cutting mat

Drinking glasses

Thick tracing paper

Glue or double-sided tape

Tea lights

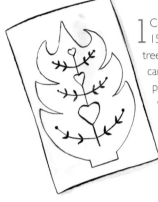

1 Copy the templates on pages 152 and 153 and cut out the tree and house shape from thin card or thick paper. Transfer the pattern onto the tree and the windows and door shapes onto the house (see page 146), including the dashed fold lines.

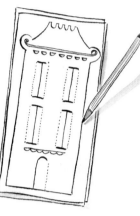

2 Use a craft knife to carefully cut out the pattern on the tree shape, cutting inside the marked lines.

3 On the house shape, score along the dashed lines, and cut along the straight lines. Fold the windows and door forward along the scored lines.

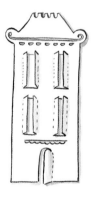

4 Measure the height of the glass you are using for your tea light. Cut a piece of thick tracing paper to this height and to a width that fits around the glass with approx. ⅝ in. (1.5cm) overlap. Glue or use a strip of double-sided tape down one side edge and join the two edges together to form a cylinder that can slide easily on and off the glass.

5 Dab some glue or attach small pieces of double-sided tape to the center on the back of the cut-out shapes and attach them to the tracing-paper cylinders. Place the tea light in the glass and slip the lantern over to finish. Alternatively, you can simply tape the paper cuts directly to the glass.

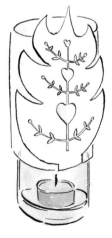

Christmas crackers

Homemade crackers add a unique festive touch to your Christmas setting. You can choose the paper to fit your scheme—and you get to pick the gifts that go inside! You can buy little charms or place a small, different decoration in each cracker. It is traditional for the cracker to contain a paper hat and a joke, but you can always decide to break with tradition and write a personal message instead!

materials

Sheet of gift wrap or wallpaper (not too thick)
Cardboard tubing, approx. 1½ in. (4cm) in diameter
Craft knife
Cutting mat
Double-sided tape, ⅜ in. (1cm) wide
Cracker pulls
Gifts, hats, jokes, etc.
String
Ribbon or trimming

1 To make one cracker, cut an oblong of gift wrap measuring 6¼ × 11 in. (16 × 28cm). Cut three sections of cardboard tube, one measuring 4 in. (10cm) long and two measuring 2½ in. (6.5cm) long.

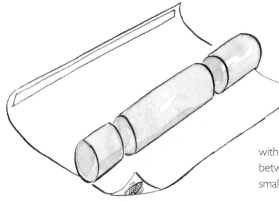

2 Lay the gift wrap pattern side down on the work surface. Place a strip of double-sided tape across the width of the edge furthest away from you. Line up the three pieces of tube across the middle of the oblong. The two smaller pieces line up with the edge of the oblong and the longer piece is centered between them. Leave a small gap in between the larger and smaller tubes.

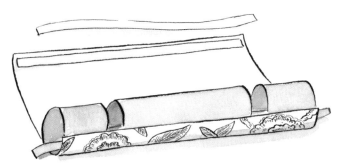

❄❄❄❄❄❄❄❄❄❄❄❄❄❄❄

Personal touches

To help identify each cracker when matching it to your seating plan, add a name label to the cracker. This is especially important if you have chosen individual gifts to suit each recipient.

3 Place the cracker pull in the tubes so that it emerges equally on each end. Put the gift and anything else in the middle tube. Peel the backing from the double-sided tape and roll the paper around the tubes until the edges overlap. Press along the double-sided tape strip to secure in place.

4 Wrap a small piece of string around the paper in the gap between the large and small piece of tube on one side. Overlap the string and pull slowly and firmly. Remove the string and the small end tube. Repeat for the opposite end of the cracker. Keep the small tubes to use for the next cracker.

5 Tie a piece of ribbon or trimming to the cracker to finish. If using ribbon around the ends, don't tie it too tightly or the cracker may not pull apart successfully.

Table runner

Create a lovely light and elegant table setting with a white table runner, simply embroidered with a pretty red heart. With the addition of a little foliage and festive candles down the center of the table, you have a warm and welcoming Nordic look to host your celebration meals.

materials

White cotton or linen, 40 × 55in.
(100 ×140cm)

Tracing paper

Pencil

Dressmaker's carbon paper

Embroidery needle

Red embroidery floss (thread)

Sewing machine and matching thread

Sewing needle

1 Fold the piece of fabric in half across its width so that it measures 20 × 55in. (50 × 140cm). Mark the center on the short edge with a pin.

2 Copy the template and design on page 162. Place a sheet of dressmaker's carbon paper on one end of the runner and position the design centered on the width, 8¾in. (22cm) up from the short edge. Transfer the design onto the fabric. Repeat to mark out the design on the other end of the runner.

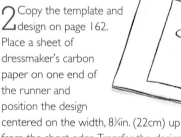

3 Embroider the design with whipped backstitch and bullion knots (see pages 144–145), using red embroidery floss (thread).

4 Pin the sides and bottom of the runner right sides together. Machine stitch a ⅜-in. (1-cm) seam all around, including along the folded edge, leaving a gap of approx. 5in (12cm) in the stitching on one long side.

5 Trim the seam allowance and turn right sides out through the gap. Pin the gap closed, turn in the raw edges, and hand stitch together using slip stitch. Press to finish.

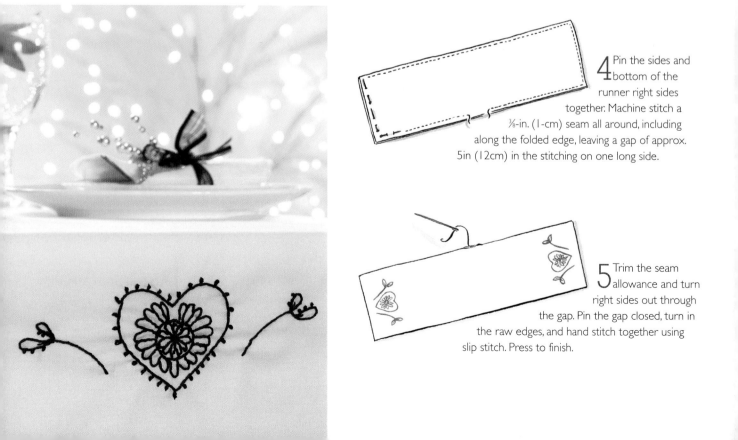

Twig reindeer

All the materials you need to make this elegant, twiggy reindeer are a few small sticks found in your back yard or on a woodland walk, and some glue. There is something very special about its simplicity. Each reindeer will be different depending on what type of twigs you can find. But one thing is certain: it will be unique!

materials

Twigs

Garden secateurs (optional, your twigs may break easily)

Quick-drying all-purpose glue

Clothes pin (peg)

1 Break off or cut a piece of twig approx. 7in. (18cm) in length and approx. ⅜in. (13mm) wide. This will form the body.

2 Select a twig that is shaped like a "Y," approx. 7in. (18cm) in height. Allow approx. 4⅓in. (11cm) of the length for the legs. Glue this piece in position at the front of the body stick.

3 Select another "Y" shaped twig, measuring 5in. (13cm) in height. The leg length needs to be the same as the front legs. Stick this to the end of the body stick, as in step 2.

4 Select two thin, twiggy branches for the antlers. Stick these on either side of the front section, on the top of the twig. You may find it helpful to secure the antlers with a clothes pin (peg) while the glue dries.

5 Select a small piece of twig that will fit in between the antlers to form the head. Stick in position.

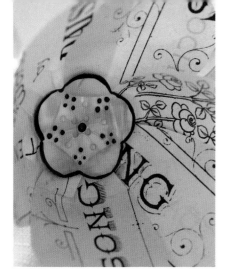

Paper flower napkin rings

A beautifully presented Christmas table really adds to the sense of occasion and personal touches make all the difference. Homemade napkin rings of pretty paper flowers and pearly buttons, wrapped around crisp white table napkins, set the scene perfectly.

materials

Tracing paper
Pencil
Scissors
Vintage music sheets or similar
Glue
Pretty pearl or glass buttons
Ribbon, ⅜in. (13mm) wide
Double-sided tape

1 Copy the petal shape from the template on page 146. Draw around the template on some old music sheets and cut out several petals. You will need six petals per flower.

2 Make a small fold in the center on the straight edge of the petal, so that the petal curls upward. Repeat with five more petals.

3 Stick the petals together with a dab of glue at the base, so that they fan round in a circle and make a flower shape.

4 Put a dab of glue in the center of the flower and stick a button in place. Let dry.

5 Cut a length of ribbon approx. 6¼in. (16cm) long. Wrap it around the napkin and tie to secure. Stick the paper flower to the ribbon with a piece of double-sided tape to finish.

Tin candle holders

These unusual candle decorations are based on the Mexican folk art of tin ware. Decorating with tin dates back to the 1500s and is still popular in Mexico today. It is a very satisfying project to work on as it is so easy, with pleasing results in no time! You can buy thin tin or foil from craft suppliers, but I use foil serving dishes that you can find easily in discount stores.

materials

Tracing paper

Pencil

Scissors

2 sheets of thick foil (available from craft supply stores or use a disposable foil roasting tin), measuring approx. 8¼ × 10in. (21 × 25cm)

Old ballpoint pen

3 candles

Strong double-sided tape or glue

3 small metal tart tins to place the candles in (you can use small glass candle holders but make sure that anything you use is very stable)

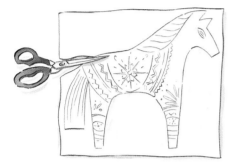

1 Copy the horse template and patterns on page 157 onto tracing paper and cut out the horse shape.

2 Lay the template on a piece of foil. Draw around the template with a ballpoint pen—an old one that has run out of ink is ideal. Press firmly to make a clear indented line. Cut out the horse shape. Take care, as the edges are sharp, and do not use your best fabric scissors as the blades will blunt very easily.

3 Lay the traced template on the foil horse and draw over the lines with the ballpoint pen, pressing firmly to transfer the pattern.

4 Place the horse next to the candle. Take a strip of foil approximately ¾ in. (2cm) wide. Bend it into a ring and use double-sided tape or glue to stick it to the back of the horse, so that it fits snugly around the candle and the horse's feet are level with the bottom of the candle.

5 Repeat steps 1–4 to make the heart and circle decorations, using the templates on page 157. Place the decorated candle in the tart tin or holder. Repeat to make two more foil candle holders.

Dancing maids cake surround

Dress up your Christmas cake with this cheerful row of dancing maids. This traditional paper cut is brought up to date with simple white paper set against vibrant orange and mirrored silver paper, for a look that is stylish and festive. Ice the cake in white and silver to complete the look.

materials
(to fit an 8in./20cm round cake)

Decorative edged scissors

Strip of silver paper, 1¾in. × 26in. (4.5 × 66cm)

Glue

Strip of colored tissue paper, 3 × 26in. (8 × 66cm)

Sheet of white paper

Tracing paper

Pencil

Scissors

Cutting mat

Craft knife

55in. (140cm) length of ribbon, ⅝in. (1.5cm) wide

1 Using decorative edged scissors, cut a patterned edge along one long edge of the silver paper strip. Wrap it around the cake and secure with a dab of glue down one overlapping edge.

2 Fold the strip of tissue paper in half widthwise and then fold under a ⅜in. (1cm) strip on the top and bottom along the length.

choose a design

Experiment with different designs and papercuts. Snowflakes would make a very pretty alternative to these dancing maids, and you could ice the top of the cake with a white snowflake pattern to complete the frosty theme. Alternatively, the horse garland featured on page 26 would work well, too (you may need to make it at a smaller size).

3 Place the tissue-paper strip around the cake, on top of the silver strip with the folded edges on the inside, centering it on the silver strip. Overlap the ends and secure with a dab of glue.

4 Cut a piece of paper 1¾ × 6¼ in. (4.5 × 16cm). Fold it in half widthwise and in half again, and then in half again. Trace the dancing figure pattern from page 165 and transfer it onto the folded white paper.

5 Use small scissors to cut out the marked pattern and a craft knife to cut the small section under the arms. Cut out inside the marked lines. Repeat steps 4–5 to make a second paper cut strip.

6 Cut a 26-in. (66-cm) length of ribbon. Wrap it around the center of the tissue band. Overlap the ends and secure with a dab of glue.

7 Put a few dabs of glue along the opened-out rows of dancing maids and stick one length on either side of the cake.

8 Cut two 13½- in. (34-cm) lengths of ribbon and tie each in a bow. Stick the bows on the band of ribbon with a dab of glue, centering them between each paper cut.

Embroidery stitch guide

This is a brief guide to the embroidery stitches used in the projects. There are many types of embroidery stitches and their variations and you can, of course, substitute stitches of your own choice.

Backstitch

Work from right to left. Bring the needle to the front, one stitch length to the left of the start of the stitching line. Insert it one stitch length to the right, at the start of the line, and bring it up one stitch length in front of the point from which it first appeared. Pull the thread through. To continue, insert the needle at the left-hand end of the previous stitch.

Whipped backstitch

Work a line of backstitches (see above), slightly longer than usual. Slide a blunt needle under the thread of the first backstitch from top to bottom and pull the thread through. Repeat in each stitch in the row.

Cross stitch

To work a single cross stitch, bring the needle up at A and take a diagonal stitch to B, come up at C and down at D.

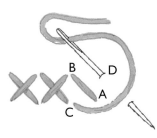

To work a row of cross stitches, work evenly spaced diagonal stitches in one direction to the end of the row, from right to left. Work back in the opposite direction, across each stitch.

Star stitch

Work a series of straight stitches from the outside of the circle to the center to create a star shape.

Detached chain stitch

To work a single chain stitch, bring the needle out and re-insert it at the same point. Bring the needle up a short distance away, looping the thread around the needle tip. Pull the thread through. To fasten the stitch, take a small vertical stitch across the bottom of the loop.

Daisy stitch

Work a group of six to eight detached chain stitches (see above) in a circle to form a flower shape.

Fly stitch

Bring the needle up at A and down at B, a short distance to the right, leaving a loose loop of thread. Come up at C, inside the loop, and down at D, outside the loop, to "tie" the loop in place.

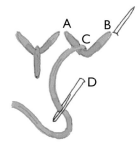

French knot

Bring the needle to the front. Wrap the thread two or three times around the tip of the needle, then reinsert the needle at the point where if first emerged, holding the threads with the thumbnail of your free hand. Pull the needle through. The wraps will form a knot on the surface of the fabric.

Slip stitch or appliqué stitch

This stitch can be used to close openings and to appliqué one piece of fabric to another. Work from right to left. Slide the needle between two pieces of fabric, and come up on the edge of the top fabric. Pick up one or two threads on the base fabric and bring the needle up a short distance along, on the edge of the top fabric. Pull through and repeat to the end.

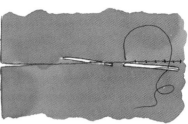

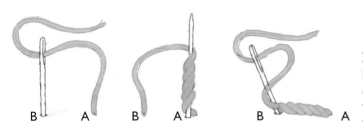

Bullion knot

This is similar to a French knot, but creates a longer coil of thread. Come up at A and go down at B, leaving a loose loop of thread—the distance from A to B should be the length of knot required. Come back up at A and wrap the thread around the needle five to eight times. Hold the wrapped thread in place with your free hand and pull the needle all the way through. Insert the needle at B and pull through.

Blanket stitch

Knot the end of the thread and bring the needle out at the edge of the fabric. Take the needle back through the fabric a short distance in from the edge and loop the thread under the needle. Pull the needle through. Make another stitch to the right, looping the thread under the needle. Continue to work along the fabric, securing with a few small stitches on the underside to finish.

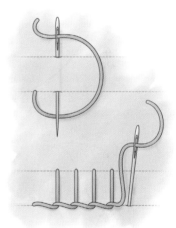

Satin stitch

Work from left to right. Draw the shape to be filled on the fabric. Work straight stitches across it, coming up at A, down at B, up at C, down at D, and so on. Place the stitches close together so that no fabric is visible between them.

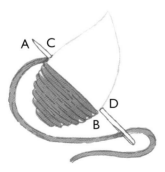

Making pom-poms

Wrap yarn 25–30 times around your fingers. Slip the yarn from your fingers, tie a longer piece of yarn around the middle of the wound yarn, and secure with a tight knot. Snip the loops on both sides and trim to the required diameter. Fluff up the fibers and keep snipping to form a neat ball.

Templates

All templates are reproduced at 100 per cent unless otherwise stated. To transfer the templates, draw around them onto tracing paper using a soft pencil, including any fold lines or stitch patterns. Place the trace over a sheet of paper or card, pencil side down. Draw over the outline with a hard pencil, pressing hard to transfer the mark. Redraw the transferred line if necessary then cut out your paper or card template to use as directed. You can either trace directly from the book, or photocopy the page first. Enlarge any templates on a photocopier before tracing, if required.

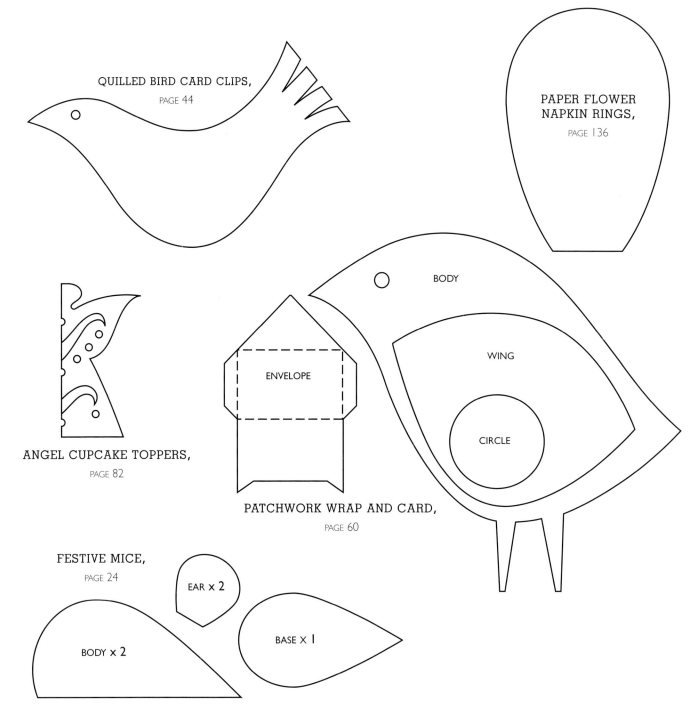

QUILLED BIRD CARD CLIPS,
PAGE 44

PAPER FLOWER
NAPKIN RINGS,
PAGE 136

ANGEL CUPCAKE TOPPERS,
PAGE 82

ENVELOPE

BODY

WING

CIRCLE

PATCHWORK WRAP AND CARD,
PAGE 60

FESTIVE MICE,
PAGE 24

EAR x 2

BASE x 1

BODY x 2

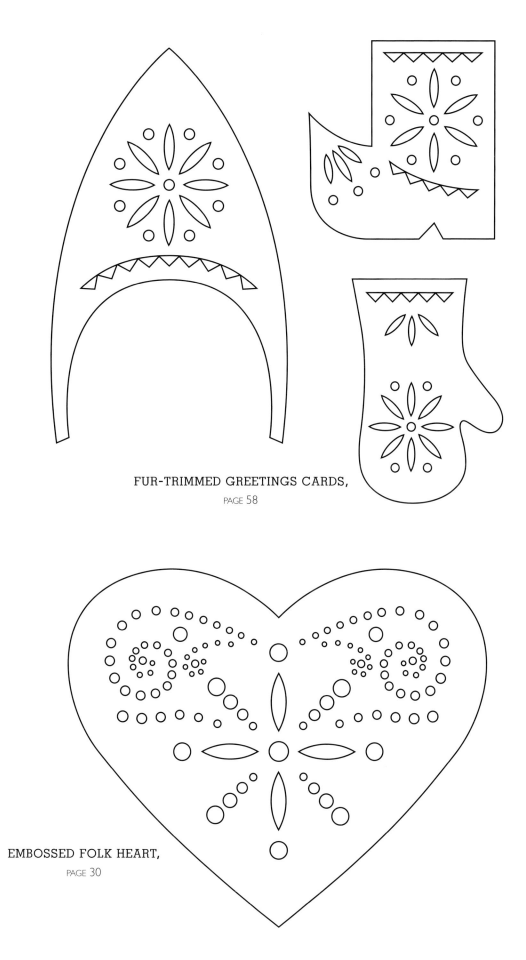

FUR-TRIMMED GREETINGS CARDS,
PAGE 58

EMBOSSED FOLK HEART,
PAGE 30

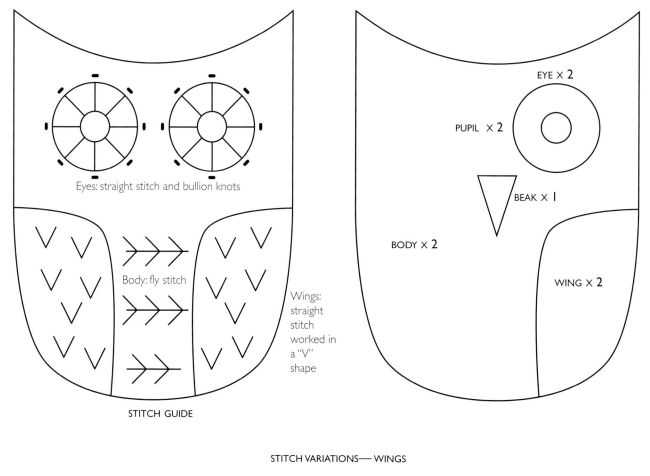

Eyes: straight stitch and bullion knots

Body: fly stitch

Wings: straight stitch worked in a "V" shape

STITCH GUIDE

EYE × 2

PUPIL × 2

BEAK × 1

BODY × 2

WING × 2

STITCH VARIATIONS— WINGS

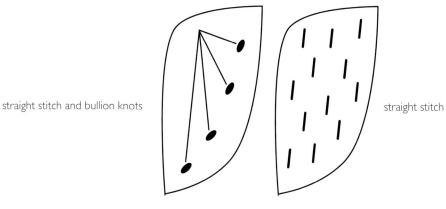

straight stitch and bullion knots

straight stitch

FELT OWL,

PAGE 18

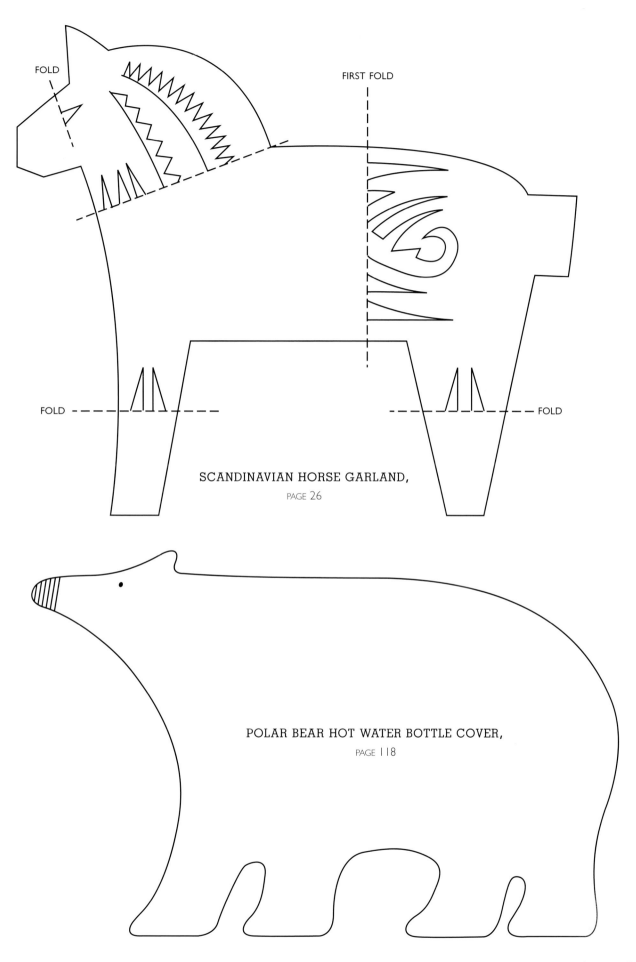

FOLD

FIRST FOLD

FOLD

FOLD

SCANDINAVIAN HORSE GARLAND,
PAGE 26

POLAR BEAR HOT WATER BOTTLE COVER,
PAGE 118

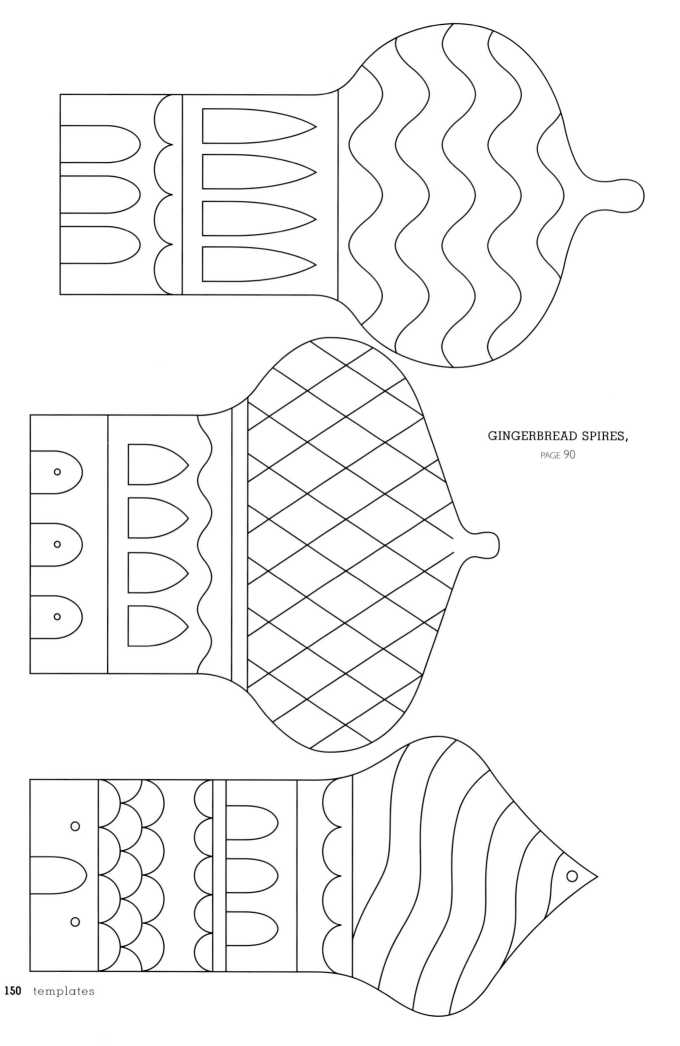

GINGERBREAD SPIRES,
PAGE 90

GOODY BAGS AND GINGERBREAD LABELS,

PAGE 64

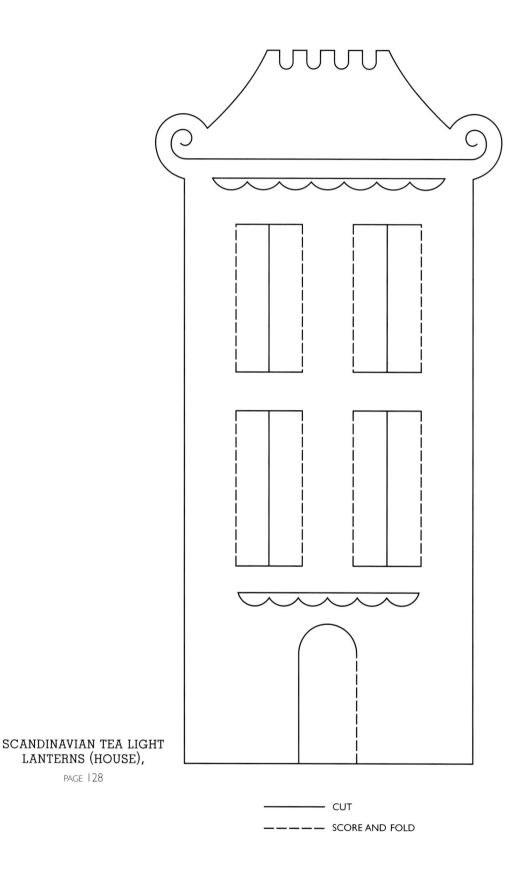

SCANDINAVIAN TEA LIGHT
LANTERNS (HOUSE),
PAGE 128

——————— CUT
– – – – – – – SCORE AND FOLD

SCANDINAVIAN TEA LIGHT
LANTERNS (TREE),
PAGE 128

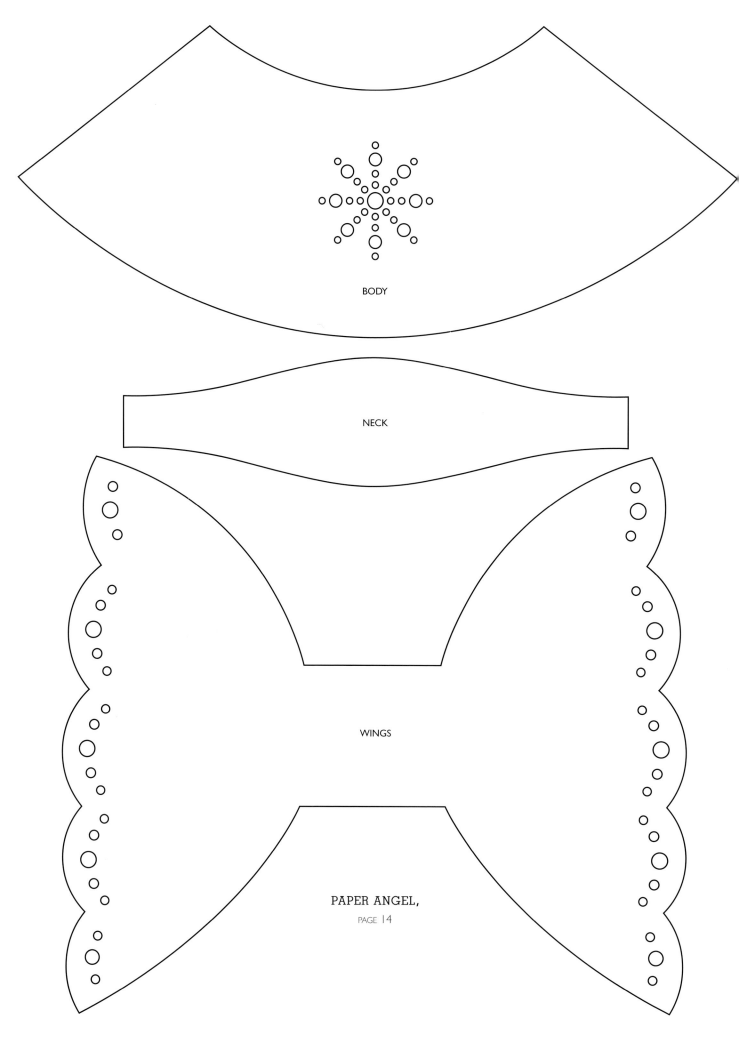

BODY

NECK

WINGS

PAPER ANGEL,
PAGE 14

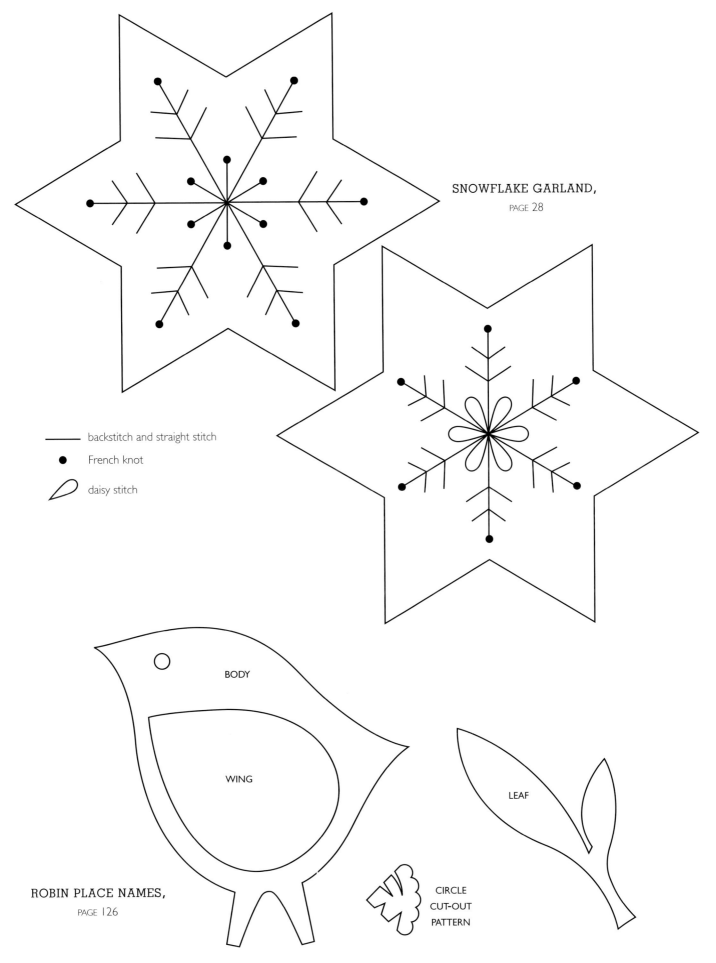

SNOWFLAKE GARLAND,
PAGE 28

backstitch and straight stitch

French knot

daisy stitch

BODY

WING

ROBIN PLACE NAMES,
PAGE 126

LEAF

CIRCLE
CUT-OUT
PATTERN

WINTER THROW,
PAGE 110

whipped backstitch ——————

bullion knot ●

TIN CANDLE HOLDERS,
PAGE 138

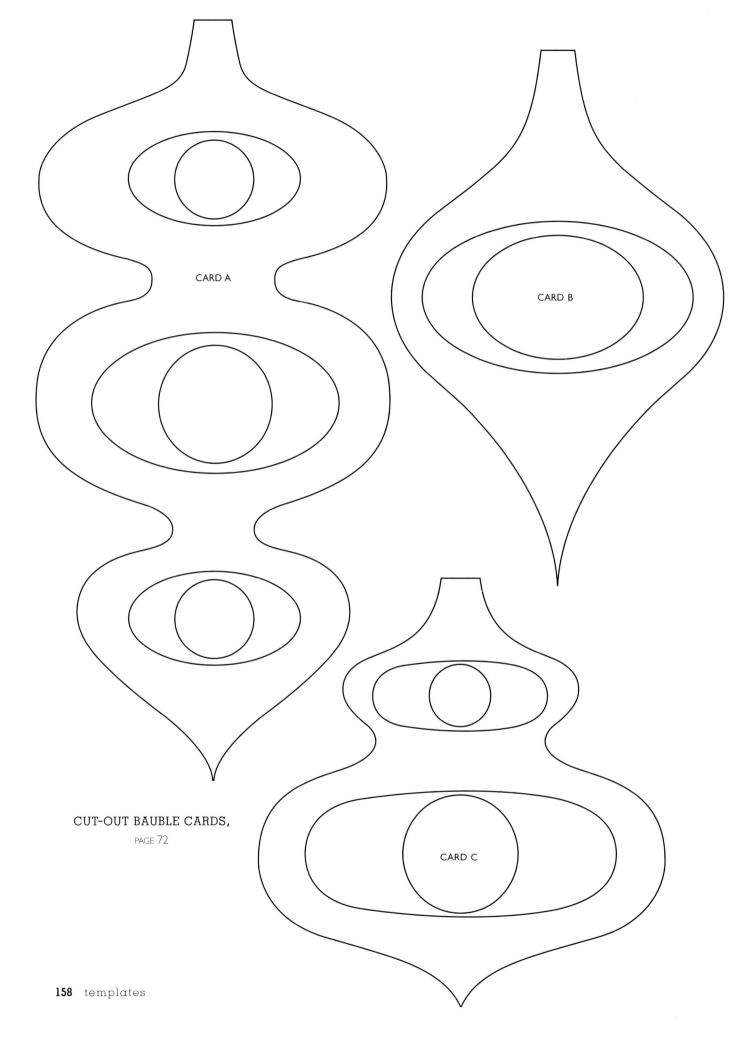

CARD A

CARD B

CARD C

CUT-OUT BAUBLE CARDS,
PAGE 72

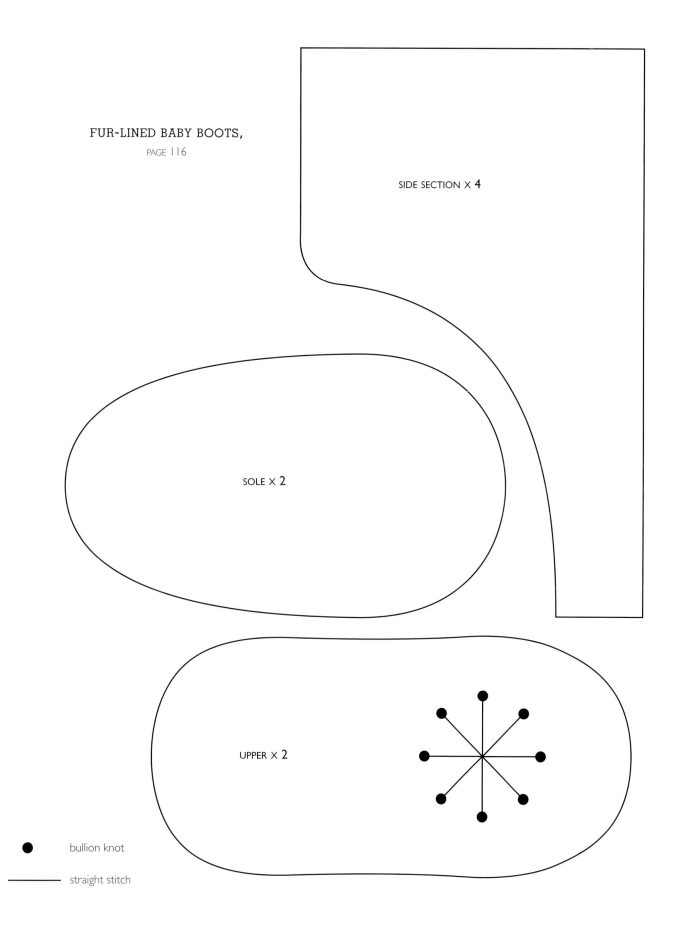

FUR-LINED BABY BOOTS,
PAGE 116

SIDE SECTION × 4

SOLE × 2

UPPER × 2

● bullion knot

—— straight stitch

PAPIER-MÂCHÉ BAUBLES,
PAGE 52

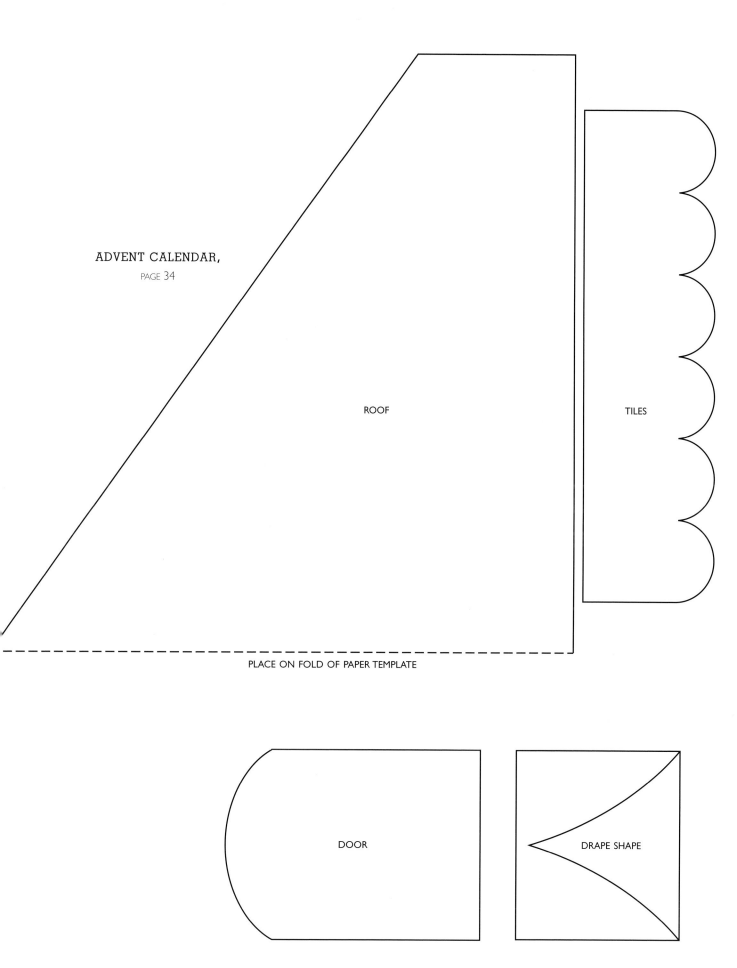

ADVENT CALENDAR,
PAGE 34

ROOF

TILES

PLACE ON FOLD OF PAPER TEMPLATE

DOOR

DRAPE SHAPE

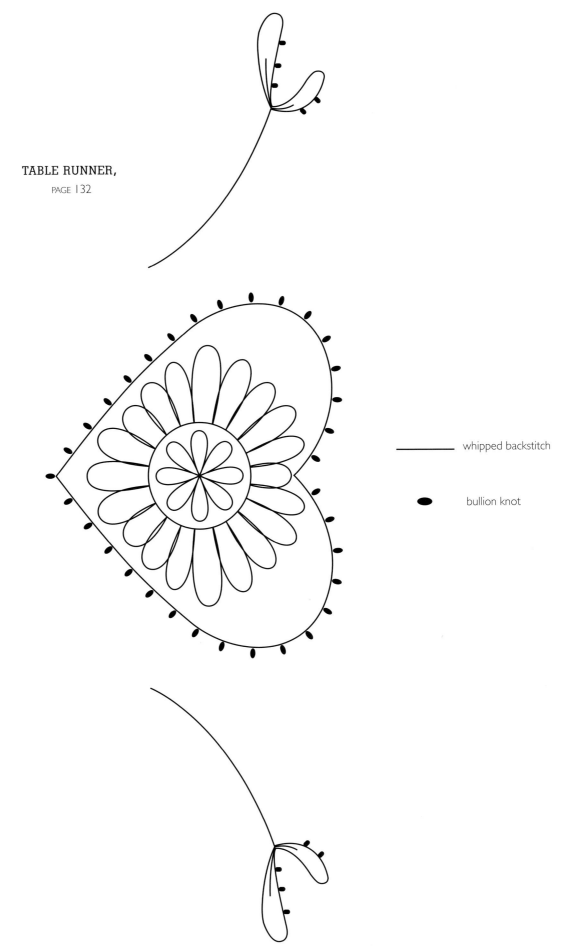

TABLE RUNNER,
PAGE 132

———— whipped backstitch

● bullion knot

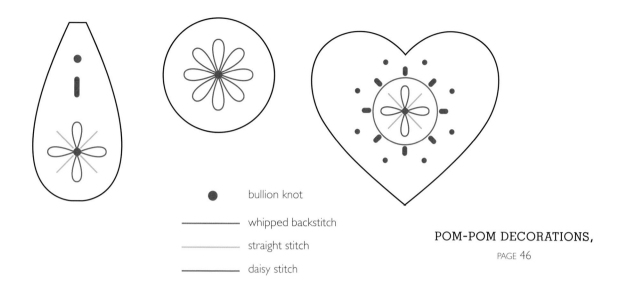

bullion knot

whipped backstitch

straight stitch

daisy stitch

POM-POM DECORATIONS,
PAGE 46

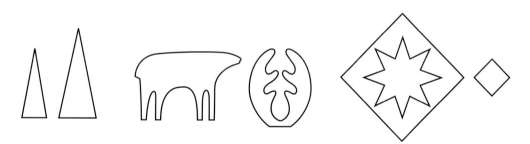

RUBBER-STAMPED CARDS,
PAGE 62

TIN BIRD CLIPS,
PAGE 32

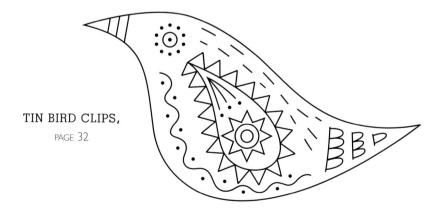

VANILLA SUGAR,

PAGE 102

LAYERED TISSUE REINDEER
CARDS,

PAGE 74

enlarge by 200%
to make the large reindeer

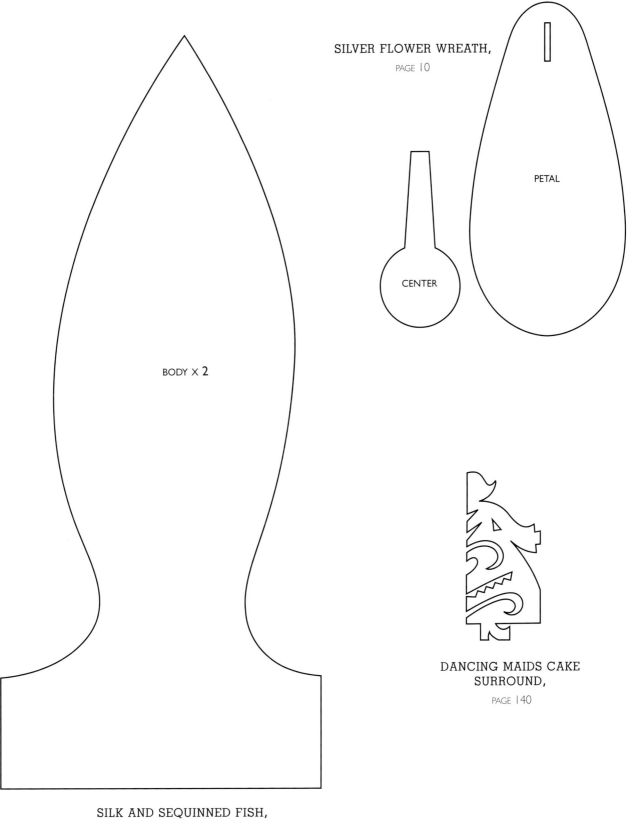

SILVER FLOWER WREATH,

PAGE 10

PETAL

CENTER

BODY × 2

DANCING MAIDS CAKE
SURROUND,

PAGE 140

SILK AND SEQUINNED FISH,

PAGE 12

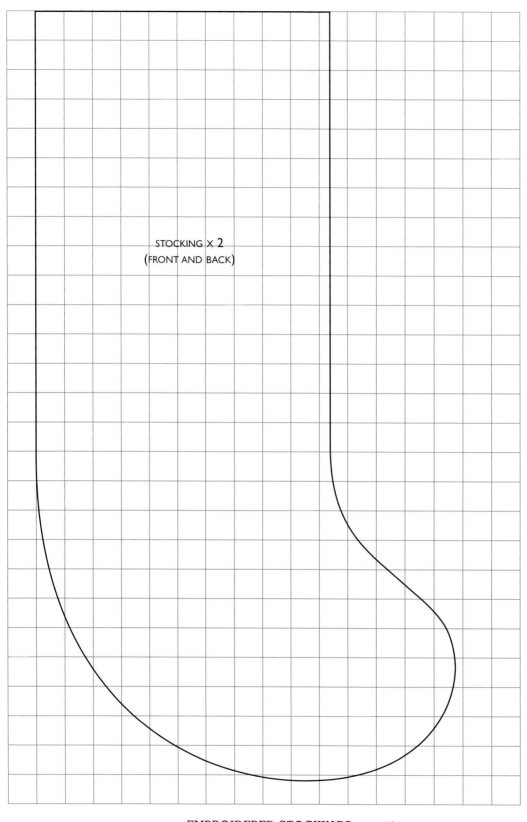

STOCKING x 2
(FRONT AND BACK)

EMBROIDERED STOCKINGS, PAGE 40

*Use pattern paper to enlarge the template to the required
size (each square = ¾in./2cm)*

bullion knot

whipped backstitch

straight stitch

EMBROIDERED STOCKINGS
(BAUBLE),

PAGE 40

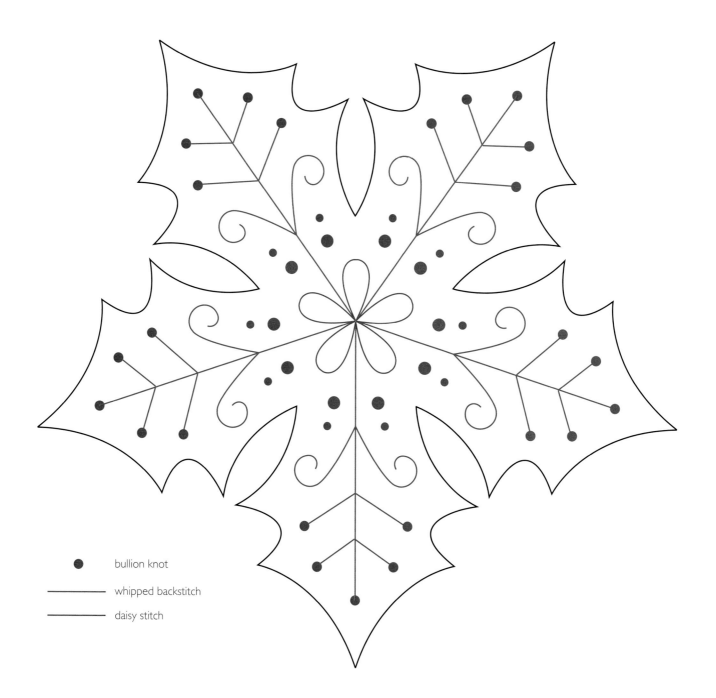

●   bullion knot

———   whipped backstitch

———   daisy stitch

EMBROIDERED STOCKINGS (STAR),

PAGE 40

EMBROIDERED STOCKINGS (TREE),

PAGE 40

bullion knot •

whipped backstitch ——

straight stitch ——

daisy stitch ——

WINDOW PAPER CUT SCENE,
PAGE 38

enlarge by 200%

CUT OUT TINTED AREAS

RUSSIAN DOLL CARDS,
PAGE 70

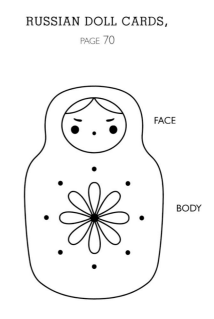

FACE

BODY

EMBROIDERED DALA HORSE,

PAGE 120

enlarge by 200%

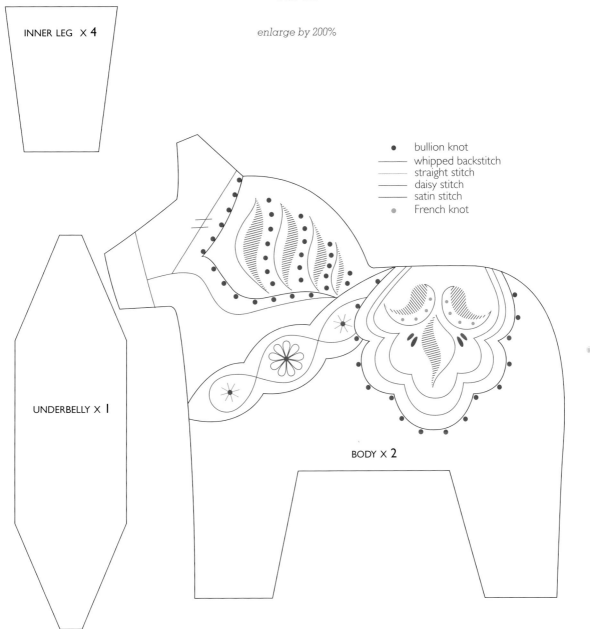

INNER LEG × 4

UNDERBELLY × 1

BODY × 2

- ● bullion knot
- — whipped backstitch
- — straight stitch
- — daisy stitch
- — satin stitch
- ● French knot

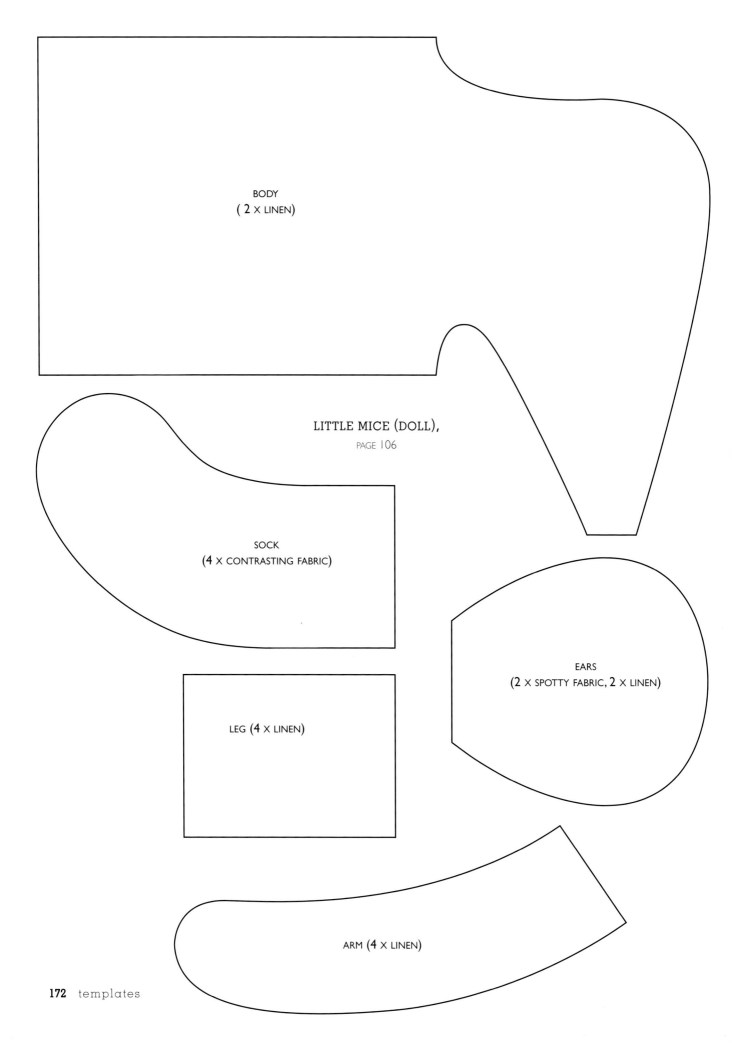

BODY
(2 x LINEN)

LITTLE MICE (DOLL),
PAGE 106

SOCK
(4 x CONTRASTING FABRIC)

LEG (4 x LINEN)

EARS
(2 x SPOTTY FABRIC, 2 x LINEN)

ARM (4 x LINEN)

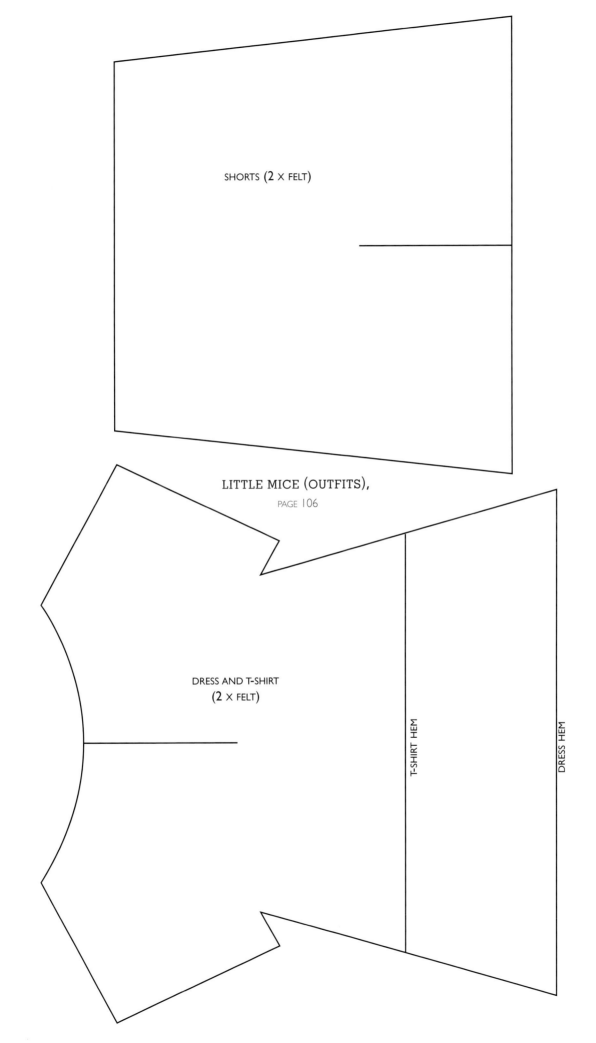

SHORTS (2 × FELT)

LITTLE MICE (OUTFITS),
PAGE 106

DRESS AND T-SHIRT
(2 × FELT)

T-SHIRT HEM

DRESS HEM

Useful addresses

US

A.C. Moore
Stores nationwide
1-888-226-6673
www.acmoore.com

Art Supplies Online
Online store
1-800-967-7367
www.artsuppliesonline.com

Crafts, etc.
Online store
1-800-888-0321
www.craftsetc.com

Craft Site Directory
Useful online resource
www.craftsitedirectory.com

Hobby Lobby
Stores nationwide
www.hobbylobby.com

Jo-Ann Fabric and Craft Store
Stores nationwide
1-888-739-4120
www.joann.com

Kate's Paperie
Stores across New York
1-800-809-9880
www.katespaperie.com

Michaels
Stores nationwide
1-800-642-4235
www.michaels.com

Paper Source
Stores nationwide
www.paper-source.com

UK

Blooming Felt
www.bloomingfelt.co.uk

The Cloth House
www.clothhouse.com
020 7437 5155

Falkiners Fine Papers
www.falkiners.com
020 7831 1151

Hobbycraft
www.hobbycraft.co.uk
0800 027 2387

John Lewis
www.johnlewis.co.uk
08456 049 049

Liberty
www.liberty.co.uk
020 7734 1234

Paperchase
www.paperchase.co.uk
0161 839 1500

The Papercraft Company
Online store
www.totalpapercraft.co.uk
07812 575510

VV Rouleaux
www.vvrouleaux.com
020 7224 5179

Index

Acknowledgments

Thanks to all at CICO Books for giving me the opportunity to write a book on such a lovely subject. Special thanks to Cindy Richards, Sally Powell, Gillian Haslam, Katie Hardwicke, and Pete Jorgensen. Thanks to designer Christine Wood, who has created such a stylish look. Thanks to Claire and James who took so much care and attention to produce beautiful photography, and to Amy for all her help. Thanks to Michael for his clear and charming illustrations and also for making me laugh so much during those busy last couple of weeks! Really special thanks to my daughters Milly, Florence, and Henrietta (my style advisers), to my son Harvey (assistant chef), and to my husband Ian, for his unending encouragement and support.